SELF-COACHING

— FOR THE —

LATTER-DAY SAINT

SOUL

LORI HOLYOAK

T0018130

CFI

An imprint of Cedar Fort, Inc.

Springville, Utah

DEDICATION

Families are the optimal learning ground for
self-coaching ☺ I'd like to thank mine for
being in the same roller coaster car. The ride
is so much more fun with each of you.

No part of this book may be reproduced in any form whatsoever, whether by graphic, visual, electronic, film, microfilm, tape recording, or any other means, without prior written permission of the publisher, except in the case of brief passages embodied in critical reviews and articles.

This is not an official publication of The Church of Jesus Christ of Latter-day Saints. The opinions and views expressed herein belong solely to the author and do not necessarily represent the opinions or views of Cedar Fort, Inc. Permission for the use of sources, graphics, and photos is also solely the responsibility of the author.

ISBN 13: 978-1-4621-4339-9

Published by CFI, an imprint of Cedar Fort, Inc.
2373 W. 700 S., Springville, UT 84663
Distributed by Cedar Fort, Inc., www.cedarfort.com

Library of Congress Control Number: 2022943166

Cover design by Courtney Proby
Cover design © 2022 Cedar Fort, Inc.

Printed in the United States of America

10 9 8 7 6 5 4 3 2 1

Printed on acid-free paper

CONTENTS

WHAT OTHERS ARE SAYING ABOUT THIS BOOK . . .

In *Self-Coaching*, Lori invites us to examine our deeply held thoughts and beliefs to evaluate what's working and what's not. Through countless scriptural examples and practice exercises, she gently guides us to begin to see the workings of our mind (and the resulting emotions and actions) in a whole new way. I believe the process Lori outlines will not only bring us greater awareness, but also help us to really know ourselves and create endless possibilities for change.

—Jaci Wightman, three-time author and Gospel-Centered Health Coach

We often talk about the what and the why—but we often find a gap in understanding the how. Having tools, like this book, to support your power of choice will allow you to live more faith focused and effective.

—Ganel-Lyn Condie, author, speaker, host of *Real Talk CFM*

Soul food. Mine, which is in a fragile place, feasted. I learned new ways to process and reframe my thoughts, feelings, actions, and results. Holyoak's blend of applicable rubrics and deep faith are a recipe for Hope.

—Kathrine, a client

These tools are life changing! Putting the work in on my own is challenging, but as I practice observing my thoughts and emotions, I have success more frequently and using the tools becomes easier.

—Diane, a client

"If your thoughts aren't serving you well, you need to change them to serve you better." That probably isn't a direct quote, but it is one of the wonderful things I learned from Lori's book! Lori's ability to connect the scripture stories we know so well to improving our thinking is amazing. She quotes from our prophet and leaders as well. I read the book and it made me feel so much better about myself, have hope for the future, and have the ability to "liken" scriptures to my own life. It's a win-win! I love her willingness to share personal stories, too. Lori has the ability to make you feel—that we are all human—that we get to feel our feelings, and that's okay. It is also okay to mess up and try again. My relationship with myself has improved as a result of reading her book. When that happens, everything is better—so much better. Thank you, Lori, for taking the time to bless all of us with your thoughtful "coaching" in this wonderful book.

—Charlotte, a client

INTRODUCTION

Imagine you've just landed at an unfamiliar airport. You've made your way to the terminal, and you suddenly spot the huge map that shows where everything is. You eagerly look for the *You are here* arrow. Once you find that, you can figure out where you need to be. And you'll know exactly how to get there.

This book is just like that map. It's designed to help you discover where you are in your life and how to get where you want to go.

Regardless of whether you already know where you are, where you want to go, and how to get there—or whether you're confused about how you ended up where you are and don't know where to go from here—the skills you'll learn in this book will benefit you.

For as long as I can remember, I have tried to make sense of the world and my place in it. I've known who I want to become, but I haven't always been sure how to get there. During those times of uncertainty, I have sought out others who have already walked the path. I've read about their experiences, tested their wisdom, and made decisions based on what resonates with me.

Let me give you a few examples. Dave Ramsey's literature helped me understand tools that would help me manage my money. Dr. Benjamin Spock and a myriad of other parenting authors taught me how to help my child establish a sleep schedule, how long to put a child in time-out, and how to handle sibling conflicts. Linda and Richard Eyre showed me how to teach my children with joy. The *Well-Trained Mind* by Susan Wise Bauer gave me a pattern for homeschooling my children. *Better Homes and Gardens* taught me how to make delicious meals for my family.

My quest for help in reaching what I want to become has included the spiritual in addition to the temporal. Throughout my life, I have searched the scriptures, looking for counsel and answers to my questions. I love the doctrines of Jesus Christ, and as one of His disciples, I am consistently seeking direction on how to apply His teachings. I love how the scriptures have taught me how to be more Christlike in my relationships with others, how to embrace my divine worth, and how to move forward with hope for the future. At times I've needed more concrete guidance to help me figure out how to apply those doctrines and principles, such as developing good habits, eating healthy foods, and using my time wisely. At those times I found supplemental resources that provided tangible tools that made gospel principles measurable.

A few years ago, I was looking for supplemental resources to improve my relationships. I knew I wanted to have eternal relationships, but I was swimming in relationship issues. I always had a good marriage but had spent the better part of our thirty-year marriage seeking more—more communication, more intimacy, more fulfillment. My husband is a very good sport. He read marriage books with me and listened patiently when I was at my wit's end. But he seemed happy and content. I knew he'd keep doing it all for me, but I also suspected he didn't think it was necessary.

One morning in January 2019, I thought, *I am done forcing him. I don't want to get rid of him, because he is a pretty awesome guy. But I have enough personal issues I can work on without dragging him along.*

You've probably heard the famous saying, "When the student is ready, the teacher comes." That's exactly what happened to me. That's when I found The Life Coach School and learned how to self-coach. Their training taught me all about self-confidence, relationship manuals and boundaries, emotional health, and so many other concepts that made gospel principles tangible.

Buddha counseled, "Holding onto anger is like drinking poison and expecting the other person to die." Turn that around: Self-coaching combined with gospel principles is like taking the antidote and watching myself get well. People who knew me didn't notice the internal struggle I was having. Most of the time *I* barely noticed. I suppressed my emotions. I tried to act happy. But inside, I was holding on to some harmful emotions.

As I started to get well, I realized some amazing things. I thought the people around me were causing me all that angst, but they didn't have to change a thing. *I* was the one who changed. I experienced what the scriptures describe as a "mighty change" (Alma 5:12–14) in my heart, and it made all the difference.

Think about how that applies to you. Maybe your emotions aren't giving you trouble. Instead, maybe you're doing things you wish you weren't doing. Or maybe you can't seem to create the results you want in your life. Or maybe you're blaming other people. Self-coaching addresses all these concerns and more.

In my journey to becoming, I read many books and studied hundreds of scriptures. This book is my gift to you, something that will do for you what many other books have done for me. It will teach you how to apply Christian principles practically so that you can join with Enos and me in saying, "My soul did rest" (Enos 1:17).

I'm not saying that you will never face a hard circumstance. That you will never be sad or angry. That you will never make a mistake and have regrets. That you will always show up as your best self. That is not the kind of rest I'm talking about, and it's not the kind of rest Enos meant.

The kind of rest I hope self-coaching will bring to you is recognizing that all the thoughts, emotions, actions, and results in your life are part of the human experience. And you can be at rest with that knowledge. You can find peace and understanding in every experience.

In this book, I combine self-coaching skills with what the prophets, Apostles, and scriptures have taught, providing hands-on tools on how to manage your thoughts, how to feel peace and joy, and how to make your efforts meaningful.

The information and tools contained in this book will enable you to do successful self-coaching, which can be beneficial for everyone. If you have unresolved trauma or other issues that feel unmanageable in your life, please seek out professional help along with the help you receive in this book.

CHAPTER 1: THE TOOL

"Every block of stone has a statue inside it and it is the task of the sculptor to discover it."

—MICHELANGELO BUONARROTI

Two-year-olds often ask, "Why?" You're probably familiar with this kind of conversation:

"You need to brush your teeth."

"Why?"

"Because it's time to get ready for bed."

"Why?"

"Because your body needs rest."

"Why?"

"So you can have a good day tomorrow."

"Why?"

Sigh.

But it's not just the two-year-old who asks *why.* Things don't change much in that regard as we get older. In fact, even as an adult, I am looking for answers to my WHYs.

"Why is this happening?"

"Why didn't I handle that better?"

"Why didn't that turn out differently?"

"Why is that so important?"

During life coach training, I learned about a tool called The Model.[1] It consists of five components:

---

1. Brooke Castillo, *Life Coach: How to Do It* (2012), 21.

- Circumstance (C)
- Thought (T)
- Feeling (F)
- Actions (A)
- Result (R)

According to the model, every facet of our lives can be plugged in to one of these components. Once we are sure of one component, we can ask ourselves questions to identify the other components. By using this tool, we can get to the bottom of all of our WHYs.

Let's look at a few examples to see how it works.

In 2 Nephi 4:26, Nephi asks, "Why should my heart weep and my soul linger in the valley of sorrow, and my flesh waste away, and my strength slacken, because of mine afflictions?"

Nephi has a WHY question. Let's plug what we know into one of the five components. As we read 2 Nephi 4, Nephi tells us that he is feeling sorrow (see verses 17, 26). We can plug that into the Feeling line of the model.

- **Circumstance:**
- **Thought:**
- **Feeling:** Sorrow.
- **Actions:**
- **Result:**

Next, we want to ask, "Why is he feeling sorrow?" In verse 17, we learn that he is thinking, "O wretched man that I am!" So let's plug that into the Thought line of the model.

- **Circumstance:**
- **Thought:** O wretched man that I am!
- **Feeling:** Sorrow.
- **Actions:**
- **Result:**

Now, what's the circumstance? We don't know exactly what happened to cause Nephi to think this way—and it's important to be factual when we explore the circumstance. Let's look at what we *do* know. We get the impression that Nephi has sinned. Here's why: In verse 17, he says, "[I] grieveth because of mine iniquities." And in verse 18, Nephi alludes to the "temptations and the sins which do so easily beset [him]." It is better to be very specific about what goes into the Circumstance line when building our own models, but since we cannot know exactly what Nephi is referring to, we will just indicate that he seems to have been involved in some kind of sin.

- **Circumstance:** Sin.
- **Thought:** O wretched man that I am!
- **Feeling:** Sorrow.
- **Actions:**
- **Result:**

Now we want to know what Nephi does when he is feeling sorrow. Still, in verses 17–19, we learn that Nephi does some self-judgment by calling himself a "wretched man," he grieves, and his "heart groaneth." So, let's plug those into the Action line of the model.

- **Circumstance:** Sin.
- **Thought:** O wretched man that I am!
- **Feeling:** Sorrow.
- **Actions:** Self-judgment, grieves, heart groans.
- **Result:**

Verse 18 also provides the result of his actions. There we read that Nephi finds more evidence "of the temptations and the sins which do so easily beset" him.

- **Circumstance:** Sin.
- **Thought:** O wretched man that I am!
- **Feeling:** Sorrow.
- **Actions:** Self-judgment, grieves, heart groans.
- **Result:** Find more evidence that I am a wretched man.

With all of this information, Nephi's WHY question may be, "Why do I keep doing what I am doing when I know what I know?"

As was the case with Nephi, the answer for most of our issues lies in the way we are thinking. We get stuck in a cycle of thinking the same way. The thinking then perpetuates an emotion. Emotion drives our repetitive actions. Through those actions, we keep getting the same results in our lives. You can see, then, how the model builds on itself: A thought creates a feeling that inspires actions that creates a result.

Let's look at a modern-day hypothetical story that parallels Nephi's model. Please understand that I am in no way suggesting that this was Nephi's sin. For all we know, his sin could have been raising his voice or getting angry at his brothers. But let's construct a model based on a sin that has become all too common in our day.

- **Circumstance:** Looked at pornography for thirty minutes.
- **Thought:** I am despicable.
- **Feeling:** Sorrow.
- **Actions:** Self-judgment, grieves, heart groans.
- **Result:** I have hate and contempt for myself.

This hypothetical person's WHY question may be, "Why do I keep doing what I am doing when I know what I know?" And the answer to his question is shown in his result. When we have contempt for ourselves, we do not value our worth. So, we keep asking the WHY questions:

"Why does it matter? "

"Why will it hurt if I do it again because I am already worthless?"

We stay stuck in this cycle of repetitive thoughts and results.

But Nephi was able to turn it around. How? Again, the power lies in our thinking. Nephi asks himself more WHY questions.

"Why should my heart weep?"

"Why should my soul linger in the valley of sorrow?"

"Why should my strength slacken?"

"Why should I yield to sin?"

"Why should I give way to temptations, that the evil one have place in my heart to destroy my peace and afflict my soul?"

"Why am I angry because of my enemy?"

Then Nephi answers his question and creates a new model for himself:

- **Circumstance:** Sin.
- **Thought:** I will "give place no more for the enemy of my soul" (2 Nephi 4:28).
- **Feeling:** Rejoice.
- **Actions:** Praise the Lord, do not slacken my strength, broken heart, contrite spirit, walk in the path and the plain road, escape my enemies, trust God, ponder on the things I have seen and heard.
- **Result:** I am no longer an enemy to myself.

Many times, we think our circumstance is our enemy. We like to blame the food in the cupboard for our weight gain. We like to blame our unhappiness on the way others treat us. We like to accuse our temptations of being our enemy. But a lot of times, our thoughts are our own worst enemy.

In those few verses in 2 Nephi 4, nothing changed in Nephi's life but his thinking. Was he a wretched man? Was he the man to whom the Lord showed "great and marvelous works"? Or was he both? He was one man who had both thoughts. One thought created sorrow, and one thought created rejoicing. Experiencing this kind of dissonance—a situation in which our thoughts create two different extremes—is an example of our brain doing what it does best. Our brain works constantly to offer us clues, reasons, and solutions to whatever is perplexing us.

Thousands of thoughts come at us every day. We have a responsibility to pay attention and choose wisely which thoughts we want to entertain. The model is a tool that allows us to separate our thoughts and examine them on an individual basis. By inserting a thought into the model, we construct a clear picture of the results stemming from the thought. The model allows us to look at our thoughts, feelings, actions, and results through a microscopic lens. As you read each chapter of this book, you will understand why looking at each component individually and collectively through closer examination is a game-changer.

The beauty of the model is that it creates awareness in our personal lives. When we can dissect an experience and compartmentalize all the pieces into one of five places, the way we create the result becomes apparent. Powerful enlightenment occurs when we choose what we want to think so we can create the results we want in our lives. Nephi's two thoughts show how he created increasingly different results: He could fuel the wretched man, or he could no longer regard himself as his enemy.

At the beginning of 2 Nephi 4, Lehi tells Laman that the Lord God "will be merciful unto you and unto your seed forever" (2 Nephi 4:7). Lehi knew all that Laman had done. He had seen the future and knew what would happen to his posterity. Yet he still offered this blessing. We can choose to believe the Lord is merciful, or we can choose to believe that we are too sinful to receive His mercy. Both beliefs are available.

So why not choose the belief that will bring us the results we want in our life?

Pause for a moment, take some time, and answer this question for yourself. Maybe you came up with some of these reasons:

1. It's easier to blame something or someone else for our situation than to take responsibility.
2. It is easier to stay stuck and complain than to make necessary changes.
3. My belief has become my truth, so I don't even recognize that I have the option of believing something different.
4. I can't just choose to believe whatever I want.
5. Everyone will know I am just faking it.
6. I may be wrong about it.
7. Just because I believe it does not make it true.

These thoughts and beliefs are available, but they might keep you stuck in a life that consistently produces results you don't want. As just one example, believing that you are too sinful to receive mercy is going to get you a completely different result than believing in the Lord's mercy.

Look at the list above and then use the model to examine each of those thoughts. Question why your brain wants to go to "I may be wrong about it" instead of "I may be right about it." Then pay attention to the answers you get.

Be curious. Bring the same desire to learn about what is going on in your own life as a two-year-old brings to the world when it starts opening up for him or her. You don't need to judge or compare. A two-year-old is not judging himself for not knowing this information sooner. He is not concerned with how this has set him back. He is not concerned with how much more his friend knows than he does. He doesn't mope around thinking someone should have taught him this already. He is not worried about whether he is asking inappropriate questions. He just wants to know WHY. Why do we call the sky blue? Why does Daddy have to go to work? Why did Joey take his toy?

The WHYs are for the sole purpose of seeking answers. Just be curious. Break the issue down into manageable pieces that can bring awareness.

Early philosophers taught the importance of awareness. Socrates said, "True wisdom comes to each of us when we realize how little we understand about life, ourselves, and the world around us."

The scriptures are replete with invitations to examine our lives. A careful study of Alma 5 provides many questions for introspection.

"Have ye experienced this mighty change in your hearts?" (Alma 5:14).

"Do you exercise faith in the redemption of him who created you?" (Alma 5:15).

"Could ye say, if ye were called to die at this time, within yourselves, that ye have been sufficiently humble?" (Alma 5:27).

We are metaphorically blind when we choose to continue going through repetitive motions that do not create great results. We mechanically choose to keep our same habits, to remain stuck, to live miserably rather than pausing to look for new perspectives, for light and knowledge, for new insights. Introspection brings awareness. Awareness allows the scales to fall from our eyes so that we may receive "sight forthwith" (Acts 9:18). When we start asking the right questions, we begin to experience awareness. And receiving sight, or awareness, is the first step of self-coaching.

Living in a time when there is information overload and when it is very challenging to determine truth, I find Saul of Tarsus's experience very interesting. He went from believing that Jesus was a blasphemer and that followers of Christ needed to be eliminated to believing that He was "a chosen vessel unto [Christ], to bear [His] name before the Gentiles, and kings, and the children of Israel" (Acts 9:15). Talk about a 360-degree change in belief!

I experienced a change in belief when it came to Saul. I always thought he was just a "bad guy." I never considered that he loved his religion and did not want to see it defiled. I didn't realize he "was an able scholar, a forceful controversialist, an ardent defender of what he regarded as the right, and a vigorous assailant of what to him was wrong."[2] Saul was living his life, believing his story, just like all of us are doing.

Our experiences in life accumulate to help us make sense of the world. They form our belief system. Then we tend to be drawn to situations that support that belief system. We acquire more evidence. After enough evidence, we stop questioning those beliefs and come to accept them as fact. Lawrence E. Corbridge addressed the side effects that "belief bias" may produce when we confront "the thought that everything one has believed and been taught may be wrong, particularly with nothing better to take its place."[3]

When we entertain going against our long-held beliefs, we experience gloom, fear, worry, and a range of other emotions. The unknown seems more daunting. But examining our beliefs and looking closely at what they are creating can provide the catalyst we need to make necessary changes or confirm that what we are doing is working.

Perhaps putting the parable "of a certain rich man" (Luke 12:15–20) into the model will help demonstrate how we can use it to uncover our beliefs and bring awareness.

---

2. James E. Talmage, *Jesus The Christ* (Salt Lake City: The Church of Jesus Christ of Latter-day Saints, 2006).

3. Lawrence E. Corbridge, "Stand on the Rock of Revelation," *Ensign*, October 2020.

- **Circumstance:** Room to store items.
- **Thought:** I will pull down my barn and build an even bigger one.
- **Feeling:** Certain. (*Note:* While I am not sure of the exact feeling of the rich man, he seemed pretty certain he was doing the right thing.)
- **Actions:** Ease, eat, drink, and be merry.
- **Result:** My "life consisteth in the abundance of the things which [I] possesseth."
- The rich man's life experiences had taught him that if you have more stuff, you should build more room to accommodate it all. That was his belief.

As we did with Nephi's example, let's do an imaginary modern-day example. I cannot provide for my family. There is never enough money to pay the bills and feed my family. Getting a second job will help me better provide for my family.

- **Circumstance:** Money.
- **Thought:** This second job will help me better provide for my family.
- **Feeling:** Burdened.
- **Action:** Work eighty hours a week, sleep four hours a night, snap at my family when I am awake, leave the house before my family wakes up in the morning, get home after the children are in bed, watch television to relax.
- **Result:** I provide for my family financially but not in other ways (emotionally, physically, spiritually).

This man's life experience helped form the belief that providing for his family financially was a priority. I'm not disputing that. In fact, I'm not discrediting either belief. Accumulating more wealth and financially providing for your family are two viable beliefs. What I *am* doing is endorsing the model as a tool to help you uncover the truth. It is a tool that will help you determine if your belief is supported by your results.

What are some of your beliefs that are not creating the results you want in life?

Maybe one of your peers in elementary school called you stupid. You believed him, and then you started to find evidence to support that belief. Then you've spent the majority of your life believing you are stupid because you never slowed down enough to question that premise. And here's why that is so damaging: That belief about yourself affects what you pursue or avoid pursuing in life.

Perhaps you were given food to comfort you, reward you, or relieve boredom. Now you believe the purpose of food is to fulfill these needs. You lost the spelling bee; let's get ice cream. You won the soccer game; let's get ice cream.

You pass these beliefs on to your children, who then pass them on to their children.

Or maybe you're like Saul. You've become firm in your conviction of "I'm right. You're wrong." As a result, you don't take time to stand back and look in the mirror and examine yourself.

Awareness creates clarity on what is causing the positive and negative results in your life. Without awareness, you likely live your life on auto-pilot. You don't slow down long enough to explore why things aren't going the way you hoped they would.

Striving for awareness can be scary, because maybe you know it's not going to be pretty to find out that your thoughts are the cause for your problems. Articles describe various stages we go through during growth and development as well as grief; some of those include denial, awareness, angst, guilt, disappointment, responsibility, ownership, and empowerment. I'm going to walk you through an example of some of the stages I experienced when doing thought work so you can see how it works.

- **Thought:** Because of hormones, I am cranky once a month.
- **Denial:** I can't control how I behave. My hormones are out of whack.
- **Awareness:** You mean there are other people who experience this and they don't act cranky?
- **Angst/Discomfort:** I wish I wouldn't have been so short with my family.

- **Shame:** I should have known better than to lash out like that.
- **Disappointment:** Now that I know I'm in control, I can't believe I'm not behaving better.
- **Responsibility:** I don't have to react with unkind words.
- **Ownership:** I can choose a new thought. I am in charge of how I speak to others when I don't feel well.
- **Empowerment:** Now that I know I am in charge of my thoughts and feelings and actions, I don't even have the desire to act cranky. I can choose a better way to think, feel, and behave.

I wove a story that I continued to tell myself and then accepted my story as fact. My story was, "Because of hormones, I am cranky once a month." That belief was played out monthly in performance after performance until I was able to question my story and find alternative thoughts that were equally believable, such as, "I am in charge of how I speak to others when I don't feel well." Those alternative thoughts served me better. They served my family better too. The model helped me take my thoughts from denial to empowerment.

This is a process, and it doesn't happen overnight. I couldn't have rapidly and automatically gone from "Because of hormones, I am cranky once a month" to "I don't have the desire to act cranky." Using the tool brought me to awareness. The new insight brought me to the door of questioning my belief. From there I was able to ask myself questions about that belief, to start practicing new thoughts that were believable but I had not chosen to entertain, and to ultimately finding a thought that was believable and also helped me feel better (see Appendix: Thought Ladder). Then I acted more in alignment with who I wanted to be, which eventually brought about a more favorable result.

The scriptures have many examples of individuals who gained awareness and changed their path because of their increased knowledge. Maybe temptation will turn our thoughts to a better way, as it did for Adam and Eve when they chose to eat the fruit and the "eyes of them both were opened" (Genesis 3:7). Perhaps after years of following in the traditions of our fathers, we may be "convinced

[to] lay down [our] weapons" (Helaman 5:51) of thought. Joseph Smith's reading of James 1:5 led to a chain of events that unraveled the confusing thoughts besetting him. Your catalyst for awareness might come from the words of a prophet, a friend, a temptation, the whisperings of the Spirit, or something you read. Or it may come from pausing to examine your thoughts. To lay them aside one by one. To take the first, necessary step of awareness.

Examining individual thoughts that are causing pain is a great starting point. As we become aware of the thoughts that are creating our emotions that are driving our actions, we discover the cause. Of course, our thoughts are not the only component that can bring awareness. We can find awareness in our feelings and actions too.

In the rest of this book, I'll teach you how to fill in the model, something that will lead to greater awareness. Only with that awareness are you able to take back the power to accept or change your experience.

This book will not tell you the answers to your questions or how to live your life. Each of us is entitled to personal revelation. The answers you need are within you. Self-coaching gives you the tools to uncover the answers within so that you can live your life with purpose and intention.

A *tool* is defined as a "device that aids in accomplishing a task."[4] Since the beginning of time, our lives have been inundated with tools to accomplish tasks. Genesis tells us that Adam and Eve "sewed fig leaves together" (Genesis 3:7) and "till[ed] the ground" (Genesis 3:23). As their posterity increased, we learn of tents, musical instruments, metal work, and an enormous ark being built.

If we use tools for their intended purpose, we get the results we want. And when we use tools purposefully, we get the results we planned for. A couple of years ago, my husband and I laid rough-cut fir planks for flooring in our house. We used a chop saw, a table saw, a flooring air nailer/stapler, a hammer, glue, and a tape measure to aid us in the process. We now enjoy a beautiful, durable floor that turned out just the way we hoped it would.

---

4. Merriam-Webster (2021) tool. In: merriam-webster.com, Available at: https://www.merriam-webster.com/dictionary/tool.

One of the tools in the Book of Mormon is the Liahona. Its purpose was to show Lehi's family the direction to go, leading them to "the more fertile parts of the wilderness" (1 Nephi 16:16). For the Liahona to work properly, Lehi and his family needed to follow the rules the Lord gave them. In the same way, the model is a fairly simple tool; its purpose is to help you gain awareness. That's it. As with the Liahona, you need to follow certain rules if you want it to work properly. There are some common mistakes people often make, which I'll address throughout the book, but essentially, simply use your common sense and intuition as you utilize it for the proper purpose. When you're building something, you might be tempted to improvise. For example, you might want to use a screwdriver as a hammer if you get desperate. Avoid that kind of temptation as you use the model.

Don't use the model inappropriately. It's not intended to judge, berate, or compare. Here's an example of how the model could be used improperly:

- **C:** I attended a neighborhood barbecue.
- **T:** I don't want to speak up because I might say something stupid.
- **F:** I feel inadequate.
- **A:** I keep silent, suppress what I want to say, and don't contribute to the conversation.
- **R:** I show a lack of intelligence.

If you're using the model above to judge, you might look at your thought (*I don't want to speak up because I might say something stupid*) and judge it with another thought—*My thought isn't even rational.*

If you're using the model above to berate, you might use it against yourself by thinking, *I am inadequate. I can't believe I didn't say anything all night.*

If you're using the model above to compare, you might think, *Everyone else had amazing things to say.*

Remind yourself that the total purpose of the model is *awareness*. When you attach a bunch of thoughts to the items in the model, you tell yourself a story. Your goal is *not* to create more stories. Your goal is to create awareness.

When you think *I want to avoid looking stupid*, you feel inadequate. When you feel inadequate you don't speak up and you withdraw. The result is you show a lack of intelligence. That's not a story—it's a recipe. Just like the recipe for a s'more: put a couple of marshmallows and a chocolate bar between two graham crackers. The recipe for the model is exactly that simple: When you think a certain thought, you feel a specific emotion, and then you act a certain way, which creates a distinct result.

Once you're aware, you can consciously decide if you want to change the recipe. If you want to try a new thought. If you want to keep the emotion. If you want to act differently. But there is no need to judge, berate, or compare. That involves using the tool for harm.

Sometimes you use tools for harm unintentionally. You burn your hand on a hot pan. You hit your thumb with a hammer. You sled into a tree. Other times, you may *intentionally* use tools for harm. You use your words to slander another person. You take too many prescription drugs. You overeat for comfort. Whether it's intentional or not, the bottom line is this: Using tools improperly won't get the results that will help you achieve your best life.

Here's another WHY question for you: Why do you even want awareness?

Awareness gives you a leg up. Awareness gives you knowledge. Awareness is the first step toward change. Samuel taught the Nephites "that as many of them as are brought to the knowledge of the truth . . . bringeth a change of heart unto them" (Helaman 15:7). In a 1993 general conference address, Elder F. Enzio Busche said, "The only way to find truth is through uncompromising self-education toward self-honesty to see the original 'real me.'"[5]

If you are not willing to examine your life, you live in oblivion to the role you play in your experiences—and, consequently, the way you feel and the things you do. The model reveals what you are creating in life. From that place, you can decide if a change needs to occur.

---

5. F. Enzio Busche, "Truth is the Issue," *Ensign*, November 1993.

CHAPTER 2: CIRCUMSTANCE

"The greater part of our happiness or
misery depends upon our dispositions,
and not upon our circumstances."

—MARTHA WASHINGTON

Everyone loves a good story. I'm sure you're no different, so here's one for you. Once upon a time, my mother-in-law came for a visit. She is always finding things wrong with me, and that day was no different. She had been in my home only long enough to sit on the couch and stick her hand down between the cushions. She pulled up some dry cereal, some candy wrappers, and a small toy. She proceeded to say [insert judgmental voice here], "Look what I found." Before the visit was over, I learned [insert patronizing voice here] that my bathroom smelled like urine, the outside of my windows needed cleaning, I shouldn't leave the dishes in the sink overnight, there was a more efficient way to cut celery . . . and a hundred other things.

I've told a hundred stories like these over my lifetime. Sometimes I've embellished them (I've combined stories from two or three of her visits). Sometimes I've changed the facts to make me look better (she really pulled two handfuls of trash from between the couch cushions). Sometimes I left parts out (my bathroom really did smell like urine). Sometimes I added snarky voices so my dear friend listening to the audaciousness of my mother-in-law would understand how unfairly I was treated and provide the empathy that made it worth retelling the story.

Let's take a look at the stories we tell. We want to be able to differentiate circumstances from our thoughts. This may seem like a simple concept, but we often weave a story around our thoughts so well that eventually they become so intertwined in our minds that it takes some conscious effort to separate them.

To see how it works, take a look at this story and assume the role of the wife:

> My husband is so inconsiderate. All he cares about is himself. He is not thoughtful about those around him. He got me into this situation. He knows how much I give. How much I have given up. The least he could do is think about my needs and be a little more considerate. If he loved me, he would spend a little more time caring about what I am going through. Thursday night he stayed up until 3 in the morning laughing with his sister. When I texted him to come to bed, he replied, "It's New Year's Eve." He came to bed at 5 a.m. He doesn't care about how tired I am. He doesn't care about how much sleep I give up taking care of his mother and the kids. When I confront him, he just gets defensive and casts the blame at me. He'd better figure out how to treat me better, because I don't know if I can stand this much longer.

The facts? My husband replied to my text, "It's New Year's Eve." My husband stayed up until 5 a.m.

The rest is a story. How do we know that? Let's break it down.

Sentence #1: My husband is so inconsiderate.

Does his sister think he is inconsiderate? Probably not. She probably thinks he is considerate. He is taking time to be with her. They are laughing and having fun. That's how we know it's a story and not a fact. When it's a story, two people do not agree that he is inconsiderate. When it's fact, everyone agrees that he is inconsiderate. It can't be a fact, then, because his sister is thinking the opposite. Why? Because of the story each person is telling herself.

Sentence #2: All he cares about is himself.

Again, let's turn to the sister for answers. Does he care only about himself? His sister would probably disagree. She is probably feeling cared for because they are spending time together. But let's forget about the sister's story for now and instead turn to your story. Is it true that he only cares about himself? You can probably find a lot of evidence to prove the validity of that statement:

He is loud.

He did not come to bed when you wanted him to.

He lets you to take care of everyone else.

I'm sure the list could go on. But is there also evidence that he cares about others? Consider these:

He let someone pull into the parking space he wanted.

He fixed a snack for the kids.

He changed the oil in your car.

You can find evidence that doesn't even agree with your own thought. That's how you know it's a story. You can do this with each sentence to separate the facts from the story. Here's another:

Sentence #3: When I texted him to come to bed, he replied, "It's New Year's Eve."

That's a fact. How do we know it's a fact? He would agree. His sister would agree. You would agree. You have the text to prove it.

Being able to separate your thoughts from the circumstances is a skill you will want to become proficient at to use the model effectively.

Here are some circumstances from my life: This week my friend's twenty-year-old son died. My eighty-year-old aunt has Covid. My daughter and son-in-law and my two grandkids moved in with us. I finished writing my personal history and self-published it. I live in Montana. The temperature today is sixty-two degrees. Yesterday I worked my last day as a part-time employee for the Church. My electric bill is $112.26.

Those are all circumstances. They are all facts. Circumstances are neutral.

And circumstances are not subjective. I can present evidence to prove the validity of each statement.

The dictionary defines *fact* as "a thing that is indisputably the case."[1] It seems we are living in a world where discerning the facts is sometimes challenging. Many people and organizations say opposing words with conviction. Our current environment is probably not much different from the culture of religious excitement of the 1820s—so easy to get "entirely lost in a strife of words and a contest about opinions" that it becomes difficult "to come to any certain conclusion who [is] right and who [is] wrong" (Joseph Smith—History 1:6, 8). As a result, people found themselves "in the midst of this war of words and tumult of opinions" wondering "who of all these parties are right; or, are they all wrong together? If any one of them be right, which is it, and how shall I know it?" (Joseph Smith—History 1:10).

Although chaotic, the 1820s don't have a monopoly on the difficulty of discerning fact. Since the beginning of creation, humanity has been trying to find correct answers. Will we die if we eat the fruit, or will we not die? What is truth? What are the facts? Are there absolute truths?

It's easy to check the dictionary for a definition of *fact*, but even then words can be open to interpretation. What makes something indisputable? Are facts based on consensus?

Let's look at a few examples. Ancient civilizations believed in a geocentric model in which the earth was at the center and the sun, moon, and stars orbited it. The heliocentric model, with the sun at the center and the planets revolving around it, is now accepted as fact. That's indisputable because of our increased understanding. But how about this? Most of the world's people believe the earth is round, yet hundreds of thousands still ascribe to the flat earth theory. When it comes to the earth's shape, the majority rules. The belief of hundreds of millions overrides the belief of hundreds of thousands. Not to mention photographs of the earth taken from outer space that clearly show a round sphere.

---

1. "Fact," *Encyclopedia.com;* available at: https://www.encyclopedia.com/social-sciences-and-law/law/law/fact (Oxford University Press, 2021).

For the most part, facts are determined by conclusive evidence and/or majority rules. A good example of that is a court of law determining someone guilty of a charge. It's a fact that the person is guilty as charged. But our brains also like to go to the outliers when labeling something as factual. Question everything. Question the majority rules beliefs. Question the outlier beliefs.

What about these examples?

Majority Belief: I have to work hard to make money.
Outlier Belief: I can earn $100,000 in six months.

If your thoughts are helping you create the results you want, then keep believing them. If not, then don't use outlier beliefs to prevent you from living your purpose. Problems occur when we label our beliefs as circumstances.

Try these on:

Circumstance: Dad had three jobs. He earned $60,000 a year.
Belief: He had to work hard.

That belief seems pretty factual, but it's just a thought. Here's another way to look at it:

Circumstance: Aunt Sandy profited $100,000 from January to June.
Belief: She is an exception.

This one's just a thought, too. Someone else may equally believe, "I can do that!"

Let's take a look at how the Bible describes the life of Job. Job lived to see the destruction of his servants, livestock, and posterity. He experienced health calamities. His friends questioned his beliefs and his righteousness, expressed disapproval of his behavior, and condemned him. Job is an outlier. Most of us will experience the loss of a pet, a job, or even a family member. We will likely have loved ones question our decisions or express disapproval of our actions. But most of us will probably not experience the losses Job did. The majority of us would probably agree that Job had a hard life. But for the sake of differentiating circumstance from fact, let's take out the outliers. It doesn't matter if your Aunt Dana, your best friend, and your employer all agree that you are having a hard time. Why? You need to separate the facts from the story. The story is comprised of the thoughts you create around the facts.

Here's how that works.

> **Fact:** You broke your arm, lost money in the stock market, and haven't seen your mother in six months.
> **Story:** You have a hard life.
> **Fact:** The apple is red.
> **Story:** This red apple is delicious.
> **Fact:** She said, "I don't like your new haircut."
> **Story:** She is so rude.
> **Fact:** John's wife left him, he lost his job, and his dog died in the same month.
> **Story:** John has a hard life.
> **Fact:** Job's wife died. Job's children died. Job's livestock died.
> **Story:** Job had a hard life.

Maybe we can all agree that someone has a hard life. But your story of having a hard life is not going to help you create the results you want. When that's your story, you focus on all the hard things. Look at Job. He had some really tough stuff happen, but we could also say that Job had a blessed life, and we could also find the evidence to prove that.

The issue is not who has the hardest life, even though we may have the data to prove it. We're not trying to learn who has the hardest life. We're trying to discover how we are contributing to the difficulty. The outcome we are striving for is to look at each circumstance with an objective lens.

Let's look at Moses 4:1–12 as an example to separate the circumstance/facts from the thoughts/beliefs.

CIRCUMSTANCE/FACTS	THOUGHTS/BELIEFS
Satan said, "Behold, here am I, send me, I will be thy son, and I will redeem all mankind, that one soul shall not be lost, and surely I will do it; wherefore give me thine honor."	Satan rebelled. Satan sought to destroy the agency of man. The serpent was more subtle than any beast of the field.
My Beloved Son said unto me, "Father, thy will be done, and the glory be thine forever."	
Satan said, "Yea, hath God said—Ye shall not eat of every tree of the garden?"	Satan sought to beguile Eve.
Eve said, "We may eat of the fruit of the trees of the garden; but of the fruit of the tree which thou behold-est in the midst of the garden, God hath said—Ye shall not eat of it, nei-ther shall ye touch it, lest ye die."	
The serpent said, "Ye shall not surely die."	The woman saw the tree was good for food. It became pleasant to the eye. And a tree to be desired to make her wise.
"She took of the fruit thereof, and did eat and also gave unto her hus-band and he did eat."	

It is always a good rule of thumb to put exactly what a person said as the circumstance. That they said it is a fact. Our belief is then what we make the fact mean. It may seem like a fact that "Satan rebelled" because the scripture states it. But *rebelled* is a subjective word, so it gets labeled as a thought/belief. More on that later.

Let's try it with a modern-day example:

My kids are so disobedient. They jump on the couch, leave their toys everywhere, and never come when I call. I must be a horrible mother to not be able to control these children. I took them to dinner at a restaurant. My daughter couldn't sit still even though I asked her to sit still a dozen times. She spilled her drink, and the waitress had to clean it up. The waitress must think I am irresponsible. By the time we left, our table looked like a tornado had touched down. It took me forever to get everyone buckled in the car and settled down. I stopped at the grocery store to get milk and bread. I let Jonny push the cart. He ran over Sally's foot with the cart. She screamed like she had been maimed. By the time I got home, I was exhausted. I yelled at the kids, "Go to your rooms and do not come out until I say you can."

CIRCUMSTANCES/FACTS	THOUGHTS/BELIEFS
They jump on the couch.	My kids are so disobedient.
I took them to dinner at a restaurant.	They leave their toys everywhere.
I said, "Sally, sit still."	They never come when I call.
Sally spilled her drink.	I must be a horrible mother to not be able to control these children.
I stopped at the grocery store to get milk and bread.	
Jonny pushed the cart.	My daughter couldn't sit still.
Jonny ran over Sally's foot.	The waitress had to clean up the drink my daughter spilled.
I said to the kids, "Go to your room and do not come out until I say you can."	The waitress must think I am irresponsible.
	Our table looked like a tornado touched down.
	It took me forever to get everyone buckled in the car and settled down.
	Sally screamed like she was maimed.
	By the time I got home, I was exhausted.

See how that works? We can clean up some of the thoughts and move them over to the circumstance side if we want a clearer picture. For example, if we wanted to move "They leave their toys everywhere" to the circumstance side, we could clean it up by stating the facts: "There are five stuffed animals on the couch, ten blocks on the carpet, and eight books in the chair."

Circumstances don't cause positive or negative emotions. Remember, circumstances are neutral. Emotions, positive *or* negative, come from the *thoughts* that accompany the circumstances. In the example above, the mother may think she is upset because her children jumped on the couch. In reality, her feelings come from her thoughts about her children jumping on the couch: "My kids are disobedient" or "My kids shouldn't be doing that."

If a circumstance doesn't feel neutral, you may need to neutralize it even more. Here's an example: Your mother-in-law said, "Your children are hooligans." To make that circumstance more neutral, you could replace *mother-in-law* with "a woman said." Sometimes we let the person who says something intensify it for us. If a stranger said, "Your children are hooligans," you might laugh it off and say, "I know, right?" Or you might think, "What does she know?" But when it's your *mother-in-law*, you ruminate over it—and it doesn't feel neutral at all.

Let's try another example. Here's the circumstance: "My father died on December 24."

I think you'll agree that doesn't feel very neutral. Besides replacing "my father" with "a man," you can help neutralize the circumstance by becoming the observer instead of the participant. If someone else said, "My father died on December 24," it would not have the same effect because it wasn't your father. Becoming an observer helps neutralize most circumstances.

The scriptures provide a great example of neutralizing a circumstance by referring to an individual as a man or a woman or by their occupation (such as a tax collector or laborer). For example, Matthew 20 tells the parable of the laborers. The laborers who "supposed that they should have received more . . . murmured" (Matthew 20:10–11). That feels pretty neutral. It *wouldn't* feel very neutral if your husband was the one who received the same wages after a full day's work as another man who was hired in the eleventh hour.

A laborer received $X is a neutralized circumstance. *My husband received $X* is also a neutralized circumstance, although your thoughts about it may create heightened emotions.

Here's another example. In John 8:3, "a woman taken in adultery" is brought before Christ. *A woman accused of adultery* is neutralized. *My wife accused of adultery* is also neutral, although your thoughts may create heightened emotions.

Bringing that a little closer to home, you can feel concerned when you hear that "one in five Americans say they've been unfaithful."[2] Despite your concern, you can feel pretty neutral about it all—*if* the one in five Americans isn't your spouse.

Don't get hung up on how neutral the circumstance appears. Just try to make it as factual as you can. Trying to see the circumstance as neutral is just another tool. If it's not helpful, don't get stuck there.

In addition to making a circumstance factual and neutral, another skill to develop is to leave out any subjective words when considering a circumstance. Personal opinions or words that might be attributed to our thoughts or mood cannot be considered fact.

Something that *seems* factual might in reality be subjective. For example, you might say, "I yelled at my kids." When our kids were teenagers, they occasionally said to their dad, "Quit yelling at me." In my husband's opinion, he wasn't yelling. See how different that is? The kids thought he was yelling; he didn't consider it yelling. Yelling is subjective based on our personal experience with decibel levels, tones, and maybe some other factors.

Let's consider again the example of Eve. The scripture said, "The woman saw the tree was good for food." She originally believed the tree was not good for food. Her opinion changed as her thoughts about it changed. Her initial thought was something

---

2. Peter Moore, "1 in 5 Americans say they've been unfaithful." *YouGovAmerica*, https://today.yougov.com/topics/lifestyle/articles-reports/2015/06/02/men-more-likely-think-cheating.

like, *I should not eat it or I will die*. Then she spoke with Satan about it. Her thought changed, and she looked at it as *a tree whose fruit will make me wise*. Whether the food was good or desirable was subjective for Eve.

I have included some practice worksheets in the Appendix (see Appendix: Separate Circumstances from Thoughts 1 and 2). The first exercise involves reading a scripture excerpt and separating the circumstances from the thoughts. The second exercise involves thinking of a circumstance from your personal life. Write down a summary of something that is troubling you. Then go back through and read your sentences. Circle the circumstances and underline the thoughts.

Why does this even matter?

President Russell M. Nelson said, "The joy we feel has little to do with the circumstances of our lives and everything to do with the focus of our lives."[3]

We like to blame or give credit to the circumstances for how we feel or what results are occurring in our lives. But that's not accurate. The circumstances, which are neutral, are not the cause of our suffering or our joy. The way we *think* about our circumstances is what creates our emotions.

Once we realize that, we get to choose how we want to interpret the circumstances. What that means is that we're not victims of our circumstances. We regain the power. The power to choose our thoughts. The power to choose our feelings. The power to choose our actions. The power to create results. The power to show up in the world as the person we are.

As Viktor Frankl so eloquently put it, "Everything can be taken from a man but one thing: the last of human freedoms—to choose one's attitude in any given set of circumstances, to choose one's own way."[4]

That's why it's so important to differentiate our circumstances from our thoughts about those circumstances. We don't get to

---

3. Russell M. Nelson, "Joy and Spiritual Survival," *Ensign,* November 2016.
4. "Viktor E. Frankl Quotes," BrainyQuote.com, BrainyMedia Inc., 2021, https://www.brainyquote.com/quotes/viktor_e_frankl_131417.

choose most circumstances in our lives. We *always* get to choose our thoughts about the circumstances.

Many people like to choose a "word of the year" or a "phrase of the year" that will help guide and inspire them throughout the year. This year I chose the phrase "Joy is mine." That's an easy phrase to roll around in my mind when things are going well, but I wanted to be able to remember it when my flight got delayed or while I was short on time and standing in a long line at the grocery store or when my heat pump broke down and cost more than $1,000 to fix. It's been a remarkable thing. I have discovered that when that thought comes to mind, I look for ways to feel joy even in circumstances I previously would not have thought were joyful. I can do this because I, like everyone else, can choose my thoughts.

Elder Jeffrey R. Holland reiterated the power of choosing our thoughts when he said:

> Learn as quickly as you can that so much of your happiness is in your hands, not in events or circumstances or fortune or misfortune. That is part of what the battle for agency was over in the premortal councils of heaven. We have choice, we have the power to make our own decisions, we have agency, and we can choose if not happiness per se, then we can choose to live after the manner of it. Happiness comes first by what comes into your head a long time before it comes into your hand.[5]

Obviously, we can change our thoughts about our circumstances. But sometimes we need to change our circumstances.

We might stay in a circumstance because it feels emotionally comfortable. Staying in the circumstance allows us to stay in our comfort zone, but it might cause us to live below our potential. For example, you might stay in a job that doesn't stretch your talents, live at home longer because you're afraid to branch out on your own, or turn down a new calling because

---

5. Jeffrey R. Holland, "The Quest for Happiness," *Ensign*, September 2016.

you don't think you have the necessary skill set. As you develop awareness about your circumstance, your thoughts, and your thoughts about your circumstances, you will be able to make better decisions about how to move forward. You will have the information you need to decide if the circumstance or the thoughts need more attention.

The scriptures give us examples of people who decided to change their circumstances. The Israelites left Egypt (see Exodus 12). The Nephites separated themselves from the Lamanites and found a new home in the wilderness (see 2 Nephi 5:5). Joseph fled from Potiphar's wife (see Genesis 39:12).

Like those examples from the scriptures, it may be necessary at times to separate ourselves from a circumstance. We may choose to get rid of all the sweets in the kitchen before starting a diet. We may choose to bury our weapons of war. We may choose to never answer the phone again when our mother calls. We may choose to cut up our credit cards. Changing the circumstance is always an option. An alternate option is to increase awareness, foster curiosity, and discover your abilities before changing the circumstance.

I mentioned earlier that I quit my job working as a part-time employee for the Church. I wanted to quit a year earlier. My hiring boss was a great administrator, and I enjoyed working for him. When he left to accept new employment, I found that my new boss was very different. I spent the better part of a year complaining about my job and my boss.

I could have easily left that job—the circumstance—a year earlier, but I'm glad I didn't. Enrolled in life coach certification at the time, I began to gain awareness of how I was blaming the job for my dissatisfaction. I started questioning my thoughts. I was curious about why I thought my new boss should do things the same way the previous boss had. I was curious why all the teachers adored him. I gradually realized the power I had to see the good in him. When I eventually did leave the job, I was in a good place. I didn't blame the job or my boss for my leaving, and I didn't feel dissatisfaction or anger or frustration. I left feeling affection for my boss and excitement for new opportunities ahead.

Changing our circumstances does not always go how we antic-ipate. Jonah tried to change his circumstance by going to Tarshish instead of Nineveh (see Jonah 1:3). After some soul searching inside the belly of the whale, he eventually ended up back in circumstance number one—in Nineveh. Maybe our circumstances, even the hard ones, are working for us, not against us. Often, as with what happened to Jonah, our circumstances can help us learn more about ourselves.

When you discover your ability to manage your thoughts, feel-ings, and actions in a given circumstance before choosing to leave, you realize the power you have in the circumstance. If you don't recognize that you have the power, you're likely to enter into the same circum-stance in the next job or the next relationship. If you're annoyed by your current boss, you're likely to be annoyed by your next boss too. If you take all the food out of your house that you consider unhealthy, what happens when you leave the house or the neighbor brings over a treat? When you know that the power lies within you to be happy at work or to make healthy food choices while surrounded by goodies, then a whole new world opens up—a world where you can change your experience simply by changing your thoughts.

We can be happy in our circumstances. How do I know? I've seen it done. I know happy people whose children misbehave. I know miserable people whose children misbehave. I know happy people who live under the poverty level. I know miserable people who live under the poverty level. I know happy people who have health challenges. I know miserable people who have health chal-lenges. President Russell M. Nelson said, "Saints can be happy under every circumstance. We can feel joy even while having a bad day, a bad week, or even a bad year!"[6]

Not sure how to make that happen? Keep reading as we exam-ine the role our thoughts play in interpreting our circumstances.

---

6. Nelson.

CHAPTER 3: THOUGHT

"In the province of the mind, what one believes to be true, either is true or becomes true."

—JOHN LILLY[1]

"Truth will always be truth, regardless of lack of understanding, disbelief or ignorance."

—W. CLEMENT STONE[2]

As a forty-four-year-old, I enrolled in college to earn a bachelor's degree in English. During a course that included identifying parts of speech, I found myself having to refer to the reference book several times. I finally realized it was no wonder I didn't remember this stuff—I had learned it in the third grade! On the other hand, I'm amazed at how other things I learned in the third grade and even younger have stuck with me. We learn basic concepts: two plus two equals four, *i* before *e* except after *c*, Christopher Columbus discovered America, there are nine planets in our solar system. (Of course, we later learn that there are exceptions to those "truths.")

It's not only the mathematical and grammatical truths that we learn at such a young age, but we hear other things that we take on

1. "John Lilly Quotes," BrainyQuote.com, BrainyMedia Inc., 2021, https://www.brainyquote.com/quotes/john_lilly_122201.
2. "W. Clement Stone Quotes," BrainyQuote.com, BrainyMedia Inc., 2021, https://www.brainyquote.com/quotes/w_clement_stone_126453.

as truths too. Those even include things about our character. I have even heard labels given to babies in the womb. When a baby was born three days after his due date, someone said, "He's so stubborn." *What?* How about, "He was so content." Okay, that's a little better label to carry around, but still . . .

What about reactions to a four-month-old who is looking around? One might say, "She is so nosy." *Say what?* Why not, "She is so inquisitive?"

Labels like that can haunt us for the rest of our lives. Imagine that someone called you "lazy" in your youth. Now, well into adulthood, when your boss questions your work ethic on a project, you may think, *That's because I'm lazy.* You choose to believe something someone said about you twenty years ago, and you continue to let it play repetitively in your head. That happens to many people.

Even Moses had a belief that he couldn't possibly be an instrument for God. "Who am I, that I should go unto Pharaoh, and that I should bring forth the children of Israel out of Egypt?" (Exodus 3:11). Because of the beliefs he held about his speaking abilities, he was sure no one would listen to him. He had a track looping in his head: "I am not eloquent. . . . I am slow of speech, and of a slow tongue" (Exodus 4:10). It was time for Moses to question his repetitive self-talk.

Let's explore WHY examining our beliefs is so important, HOW to determine truth, and WHAT is truth.

Why Is It So Important to Examine Our Beliefs?

We make decisions based on our beliefs. Those beliefs start with a thought. A thought is just a sentence in our brain. Thoughts are optional. When we grab on to a thought and continue to think it repetitively, it becomes a part of our belief system. Those beliefs become our truths, which then guide our life choices. That is why knowing the truth is so important.

For example, after being married a few months, I discovered my husband and I had very different beliefs about money. We came from two ends of the spectrum—save every penny you have to spend every penny you make. I'm not saying one of those thoughts is more truthful than the other. My point is that our thoughts were congruent with our belief systems. And those thoughts guided our behavior.

Let's look at some thoughts from people in the scriptures and at the behavior that stemmed from those thoughts.

SCRIPTURE	THOUGHT	BEHAVIOR
Naaman the Leper 2 Kings 5:11–14	"Behold, I thought, He will surely come out to me, and stand, and call on the name of the Lord his God, and strike his hand over the place, and recover the leper." Maybe my servant is right when he says, "If the prophet had bid thee *do some* great thing, wouldest thou not have done *it*?"	"So he turned and went away in a rage." "Then went he down, and dipped himself seven times in Jordan, according to the saying of the man of God: and his flesh came again like unto the flesh of a little child, and he was clean."
Lamanite Queen Alma 19	I believe that it shall be according as thou hast said that "He is not dead, but he sleepeth in God, and on the morrow he shall rise again."	She watched over the bed of her husband instead of burying him.
David 2 Samuel 11:2–15	"The woman *was* very beautiful to look upon."	"He lay with her." He sent for Uriah. He set "Uriah in the forefront of the hottest battle."
Woman with Issue of Blood Mark 5:25-28	"If I may touch but his clothes, I shall be whole."	She touched His garment.
Rahab Joshua 2:21	"According unto your words, so *be* it."	"She bound the scarlet line in the widow."

Examining our thoughts is important because our actions are in direct correlation with the thoughts we entertain. When Naaman believed the prophet should have healed him in some grandiose way, he walked away. When he believed washing in the river might cure his leprosy, he went for a dip. We experience the same patterns today. If Mom tells us not to touch the stove because we will get burned, we don't touch it if we think she's telling the truth. If we think she doesn't know what she's talking about, then we touch it.

How Do We Determine Truth?

So how do we know if Mom is telling the truth? How do we determine truth? We don't come out of the womb knowing everything. We learn as we go, "precept upon precept; line upon line" (Isaiah 28:10). As we progress, our truths may expand or change. Here's an example. Until I was in my early thirties, I believed watermelon was disgusting. One summer day I decided to try it again, and I thought it tasted delicious.

Some of the thoughts we have practiced over and over may be as harmless as disliking a fruit. Other beliefs, however, may have a deeper impact. For example, as a mother of four young children, somewhere along the way I adopted the belief that taking care of them was a higher priority than taking care of me. I sacrificed a lot of myself. When my newborn cried, I quickly tried to figure out what was wrong and what I could do to comfort her. I put whatever I was doing on hold to feed her, burp her, or change her diaper. That pattern continued as my children got older. After all, that quesadilla I was about to eat was going to have to wait if my child was throwing up all over the couch.

One day I decided to think about prioritizing my needs too. It wasn't until I started taking better care of myself that I discovered I was being a better example of beliefs I wanted to pass on to my children. I also learned it wasn't either/or—either I take care of them, or I take care of me. I learned there was balance, and I learned that I had the capability to do both.

We make decisions based on our belief system. Maya Angelou said, "I did then what I knew how to do. Now that I know better, I do better."[3] Lawrence E. Corbridge said, "You cannot be better than what you know. Most of us act based on our beliefs. . . . The problem is, we are sometimes wrong."[4] And because we can be wrong, it is important to uncover our belief systems. We can do that by looking at our thoughts.

To determine truth, we can start by questioning our thoughts. Is watermelon really disgusting? Is a mother who doesn't take care of her own needs better equipped to serve her children than one who does?

That can be a daunting prospect for you, just like it is for everyone else. It's difficult to question our beliefs. It's comfortable to keep them. The brain is a well-trained machine that likes efficiency; it's a creature of habit. Training the brain to accept new ideas takes practice because it's easier to repeat the same old phrasing than to do research, have discussions, disprove an established thought, and practice a new thought.

It's often easier to just keep holding on to long-held beliefs than to be curious or put in the work required to discover other options. But if you're willing to do the work, the long-term benefits are more satisfying than clinging to those old beliefs.

Here's an example from the scriptures. The Pharisees were comfortable and certain of their beliefs. They were rigid about following the rules, and those rules dictated with whom it was appropriate to associate, among other things. The Lord tried to show them another way. Some, like Nicodemus, were willing to question their beliefs and adopt new beliefs. Others clung tightly to their long-held beliefs.

Nicodemus demonstrated that asking questions is an important part of the process—it helps us decide if we want to hold on to our beliefs tightly or to let them go. Unfortunately, too often we are unwilling to ask questions because of the stigma. Here's how it goes: We want others to think we know everything, and if we ask a question, others might think we're too dumb to know the answer. No one wants to be considered dumb.

---

3. J. N. Salters, "35 Maya Angelou Quotes That Changed My Life," *Huffpost*, https://www.huffpost.com/entry/35-maya-angelou-quotes-th_b_5412166.
4. Lawrence E. Corbridge, "Stand on the Rock of Revelation," *Ensign*, November 2020.

Nicodemus didn't fall into that trap; he wasn't afraid to ask a question. I love Nicodemus's question as the Lord taught him about being born again. Nicodemus asked, "How can a man be born when he is old? can he enter the second time into his mother's womb, and be born?" (John 3:4). With that question, the Lord was lovingly prepared to teach him about baptism by water and by the Spirit.

I think of the numerous times I sat in classes confused but didn't want to ask a question or get clarification because I believed everyone else in the class already knew exactly what the teacher was talking about. I'm sure I'm far from the only one who's had that experience. While asking questions may label us as dumb, asking questions about our faith may label us as doubters. Let's question that belief for a moment.

For starters, the scriptures are full of questions. Cecil O. Samuelson said:

> Some seem to believe that faith and questions are antithetical. Such could not be further from the truth. The Restoration itself was unfolded by the proper and necessary melding of both. The Prophet Joseph Smith had both faith and questions. Indeed, the passage of scripture (James 1:5) that led Joseph to the Sacred Grove experience includes both a question and the promise of an answer based on the asker's faith.[5]

This quote contradicts the belief that questioning is dangerous or inappropriate.

The Socratic method of asking and answering questions has been accepted as a key teaching and learning strategy for thousands of years. Let's use the six categories of Bloom's Taxonomy and the book of Matthew to think more deeply about our beliefs as we study questions the Lord asked.

---

5. Cecil O. Samuelson, "The Importance of Asking Questions," *BYU Speeches*, 13 November 2001, https://speeches.byu.edu/talks/cecil-o-samuelson/importance-asking-questions/.

QUESTION CATEGORY	SCRIPTURAL QUESTIONS
Knowledge	"How many loaves have ye?" (Matthew 15:34) "Of whom do the kings of the earth take custom?" (Matthew 17:25)
Comprehension	"Why do . . . thy disciples fast not?" (Matthew 9:14) "Whom say ye that I am?" (Matthew 16:15)
Application	"Why beholdest thou the mote that is in thy brother's eye, but considerest not the beam that is in thine own eye?" (Matthew 7:3)
Analysis	"Are ye not much better than they?" (Matthew 6:26) "Why are ye fearful?" (Matthew 8:26) "Are ye also yet without understanding?" (Matthew 15:16)
Synthesis	"Ye are the salt of the earth: but if the salt have lost his savour, wherewith shall it be salted?" (Matthew 5:13) "Wherefore think ye evil in your hearts?" (Matthew 9:4) "How think ye?" (Matthew 18:12)
Evaluation	"Is [it] easier, to say, . . . Arise, and walk?" (Matthew 9:5) "Why do ye also transgress the commandment of God by your tradition?" (Matthew 15:3) "Who then can be saved?" (Matthew 19:25)

Now let's take a look at some modern-day thoughts and questions we can ask to gain more awareness.

CATEGORY	THOUGHT	QUESTION
Knowledge	I have so much to do today.	How many things need to be accomplished?
Comprehension	My kids are naughty.	Do they act out when they are tired or hungry?
Application	That conference talk was powerful.	How can I incorporate the principles taught into my life?
Analysis	I am a horrible cook.	Do I enjoy some meals I make? Could I get more experience? Do I want to become a better cook?
Synthesis	There is never enough money.	How can I change my budget? Can I save more? Make more?
Evaluation	My mother-in-law thinks I should keep a cleaner home.	How do I feel about my home?

Sometimes we ask questions just for knowledge. When our thought is, "I have so much to do today," we might ask ourselves, "How many things need to be accomplished today?" Asking just that one question can take us from feeling overwhelmed by "so much to do" to feeling capable enough to accomplish the "six things that must get done."

Each type of question has its benefits. For example, I already post on Instagram once a day. How can I apply that skill to writing a weekly blog? As another example, if I do not use vulgar language, I might want to evaluate why I choose to hear it in the entertainment I engage in.

If something is confusing, if something is not serving you, or if something is in the way of living a better life, a good place to start is to question your thoughts.

Just as with answers to prayer, answers to our questions don't always come the way we imagine they will. Some answers come right away; some answers come during the fourth watch. Some answers are forthright; some cause us to contemplate. The brother of Jared wondered how they were going to steer the barges, how they were going to breathe, and how they were going to see as they crossed the great sea (see Ether 2:19). He asked the questions. The Lord gave him answers to some of his questions but left him to find answers to other questions on his own. We will have that same experience.

Toss away any expectations or fears you may have because it's time to start asking the questions. It's time to start questioning your thoughts. Ask the questions that make you look dumb. Ask the questions that make you appear that you doubt. Ask the questions that will bring insight to your thought loops. Ask the questions that will help you learn and grow.

What Is Truth?

What is truth? Are there absolute truths?

A *truth* is "a fact or belief that is accepted as true."[6] As much as we want to know the truth, sometimes we are left to choose our own truth. Sometimes we just have to decide what we believe and move into it. Examples:

- My family will be better off if I take that job in Texas.
- If I ground my teenager, he will understand the seriousness of his actions.
- If I am a stay-at-home mom, my children will have a bigger advantage in life.
- If I homeschool my children, they will be safe from spiritual and physical hazards.

---

6. "Truth," Lexico.com, available at: https://www.lexico.com/en/definition/truth (Oxford University Press, 2021).

Could be true. Or maybe they're not true.

One thing the brain does efficiently is to repeat phrases over and over—even those that aren't true. When that happens, you become convinced that those things are true:

- This is too hard.
- There is no way to steer the barges.
- There is no way to navigate out of this dead-end job.
- We will not be able to breathe.
- This marriage is suffocating me.
- I cannot see in this darkness.
- The early sunsets in the winter depress me.

Those repetitive thoughts become our truth:

- He shouldn't have done that.
- That was rude.
- I am not good enough.
- I could never do that.
- I am right.

We want to believe that truth is truth. But even *that's* not always true. Why? We can have different truths. Let's examine some examples from the scriptures to demonstrate what I mean.

TRUTH	TRUTH
Daniel 6:7–10 When King Darius sent out a decree that no one "shall ask a petition of any God or man for thirty days, save of thee, O king," Daniel "went into his house; and his windows being open in his chamber toward Jerusalem, he kneeled upon his knees three times a day, and prayed, and gave thanks before his God, as he did aforetime."	**Mosiah 24:11–12** When "Amulon commanded them that they should stop their cries; and he put guards over them to watch them, that whosoever should be found calling upon God should be put to death," "Alma and his people did not raise their voices to the Lord their God, but did pour out their hearts to him."

When commanded to stop praying, Daniel chose to continue to pray vocally. When commanded to stop praying, Alma and his people stopped praying out loud but prayed in their hearts.

Ether 2:6	Exodus 14:22
The Jaredites "did build barges, in which they did cross many waters."	"And the children of Israel went into the midst of the sea upon the dry *ground*."

As we traverse the journey of life, some of us will go metaphorically on dry ground and some of us will go across the sea. We each have a different path to take. In Doctrine and Covenants 62: 7, the Lord is telling some elders that it does not matter to Him if they get there "upon horses, or upon mules, or in chariots."

Matthew 1:18	Luke 1:36
"His mother Mary was espoused to Joseph."	"Thy cousin Elisabeth, she hath also conceived a son in her old age."

Mary conceived as a young woman while Elisabeth was in her old age.

Alma 46:13, 20	Alma 24:19
Moroni rent his coat, "and he fastened on his head-plate, and his breastplate, and his shields, and girded on his armor about his loins" and invited "whosoever will maintain this title upon the land, let them come forth in the strength of the Lord."	"When these Lamanites were brought to believe . . . and would suffer even unto death rather than commit sin; and thus we see that . . . they buried the weapons of war, for peace."

The Anti-Nephi-Lehis would rather suffer death than fight with their weapons of war. On the other hand, Moroni raised the title of liberty to fight for freedom. Both groups—one choosing to bury their weapons of war and the other choosing to fight with their weapons of war—were acting as a testimony and covenant to God. They were both willing to die rather than transgress or forsake God. But that truth looked very different for each group.

Luke 2:16	Luke 2:25–26
The shepherds went with haste to see Jesus.	Simeon waited patiently at the temple for Jesus to appear.

Should we hurriedly do something or patiently do something?

We get it in our minds that there is a right way and a wrong way to do things—and we believe that choosing the right way will keep us on the "strait and narrow path" (2 Nephi 31:18). But as we can see from the examples above, choosing the right way may look different for each of us. Perhaps we refuse to eat the fruit or perhaps we agree to eat it. Maybe we bury our weapons of war or maybe we carry them into battle. Our beliefs on what path to take to eternal salvation are personal. When trying to determine truth, we should gather as much information, light, and knowledge as possible, then we should walk as guided by those internal truths.

Let's look at how that works. When Mary and Martha were hosting the Savior, Mary's truth was, "I will sit at the Savior's feet, and hear his word" (Luke 10:39, paraphrased). Martha's thoughts turned to getting ready for the Lord's visit by serving Him. I believe that if Martha had accepted her internal truth of "serving the Lord," then she would not have needed to petition the Lord to bid Mary to help her. We can use the phrasing "Mary hath chosen that good part" (Luke 10:42) to form a belief that there is a right way to do things. But I don't think that's what is being communicated to us. Mary's truth that she was going to get the most out of her visit with the Lord by sitting at His feet was not any better than Martha's truth that she was going to get the most out of her visit with the Lord by serving Him. The conflict came in the comparing.

The question we want to ask ourselves is, "What do I believe? How do I want to show up in the world?" Do your research; ask your friends what they think; seek personal revelation. Then live your truth. Elder Jeffrey R. Holland said:

> If it was right when you prayed about it and trusted it and lived for it, it is right now. Don't give up when the pressure mounts. Certainly don't give in to that being who is bent on the destruction of your happiness. Face your doubts. Master your fears. Cast not away therefore your confidence. Stay the course and see the beauty of life unfold for you.[7]

7. Jeffrey R. Holland, "Cast Not Away Therefore Your Confidence," *Liahona*, June 2000.

Problems occur when we look to see what others are doing. The multitude of opinions is not going to diminish. Discover the pattern that works for you when discerning truth.

I have a strong desire to be able to discern truth from error as I listen to all the prevalent philosophies and as I listen to my own voice. I don't want to end up on the bandwagon of something that sounds nice but is made up of only half-truths. I don't want to end up in the same predicament as Korihor allowing the devil to deceive me (see Alma 30:53). I don't want to believe things that are said just because they are "pleasing unto the carnal mind" (Ibid). I don't want to continue believing something just because it's too hard to do the work to change my thoughts. I feel a great responsibility and need to seek truth and not be led astray by enticing beliefs that seem benevolent but that mix disconcerting statements in with the relevant and meaningful.

I do the best I can to discern truth. I talk about absolute truth later in the book, but that's not what I'm talking about here. The type of truth I'm talking about here is a personal truth that has come from thoughts we continue to think. Those thoughts form our belief system and guide the choices we make. When faced with choices, I gather the best information I can and then make a decision. Sometimes that decision looks different for me than for others. Stay-at-home mom/working mom. Spend the holidays with family during the pandemic/stay home for the holidays during the pandemic. Sacrifice my time/sacrifice my money. Even while trying to make the best decision, sometimes I get duped. Sometimes I hold on to truths I regret later. That is just part of the human experience.

As we try to determine truth, we should examine our beliefs to see if they are thoughts that we want to continue entertaining. Some of our thoughts *sound* like facts. They sound noble. Beneficial. Positive.

Let's look at a couple of examples. You may think, "I should never make a wrong choice."

It sounds like a nice thought. It sounds so true. But is it? It is always a good idea to go back to asking the right questions. While God doesn't want me to make wrong choices, did He think I would? Did He have a plan for that? What do the scriptures say about it? What is the Spirit teaching me?

The Church produced a video called *Wrong Roads*[8] about a trip Elder Jeffrey R. Holland took with his son Matthew to see the Colorado River. On the way home, they felt prompted to go down a specific road only to discover it was the wrong choice. Elder Holland said, "Because we were prompted to take the road to the left, we quickly discovered which one was the right one. . . . Sometimes in response to prayers, the Lord may guide us down what *seems* to be the wrong road—or at least a road we don't understand—so, in due time, He can get us firmly and without question on the right road."[9] The Lord allows us to use our agency. Often that agency includes acting on truths, partial truths, or untruths. Sometimes the actions we take based on our belief system reveals the pathway to truth.

A family moved to our city following inspiration they received. After a year, they hadn't found employment, their previous home hadn't sold, and things were not working out like they hoped. They moved back.

Those following the Mosaic law walked down the *eye for an eye path* until the *love your enemy path* became the better option. Nephi and his brothers walked down a few paths to get the brass plates until finally walking down the successful path. For many years, priesthood ordination was withheld from men of black African descent until we got on the *all worthy males path*. For a short time, eight-year-old children of LGBTQ families couldn't receive baby blessings or be baptized. In each of these examples, the journey started down one path but then back-tracked to another path.

This life is filled with opportunities to make choices, and some of them we will label as wrong. Perhaps it is just a learning experience. Let's continue on with our "I should never make a wrong choice" example.

When we plug that sentence into the model, this is what we most likely will get when we do make a choice we deem as wrong:

---

8. https://www.churchofjesuschrist.org/media/video/2013-09-0016-wrong-roads?lang=eng
9. Matthew Holland, "Wrong Roads and Revelation." *New Era,* July 2005.

- **C:** Decision.
- **T:** I should never make a wrong choice, but I do.
- **F:** Shame.
- **A:** Self-loathing, hiding, lashing out at others verbally, comparing self to others.
- **R:** I make more "wrong" choices.

The results in our lives are a direct reflection of our thoughts. In this case, the thought *I should never make a wrong choice* leads to more wrong choices: judging, self-worth based on actions, feelings of disgust for oneself, comparing, and lashing out.

Sometimes we may decide a thought is true, but just thinking something is true doesn't serve us. In that case, we may want to explore different thoughts that are also true but that will serve us better.

For example, if I am currently unemployed, I may think, *I don't have a job.* That thought is true. Even though it's a true thought, it might create a feeling of depression. The feeling of depression could drive the actions of staying in bed, failing to apply for new jobs, or eating comfort food, among others. So while "I don't have a job" is a true statement, I may choose to think instead, *I am employable.* That thought is also true. And it might create a feeling of confidence that would most likely lead to more positive actions.

Sometimes we decide there is only one right way to think—only one correct belief. We might want to question that. Let's look at some scriptural examples.

In Genesis 3:20, "Adam called his wife's name Eve; because she was the mother of all living." She did not have any children then. Eve could have believed, "I am not a mother." Is the belief "I am not a mother because I do not have any children" true? Is that a belief to be questioned?

One way to determine the truth of that belief is to look at the definitions of words and see if our thinking aligns with the definition. *Mother* can be defined as "to give birth to" or " to care for or protect" or someone who is "a female parent."[10] In other words, there's more to being a mother than strictly giving birth to a child. Sheri Dew said, "For reasons known to the Lord, some women are required to wait to have children. . . . But the Lord's timetable for each of us does not negate our nature. And all around us are those who need to be loved and led."[11] We are *mothers* if we choose to be mothering—"caring, protective, and kind."[12]

Another example is found in 1 Nephi 2:20. The Lord promises Nephi, "Ye shall prosper, and shall be led to a land of promise."

That caused me to reflect on the word *prosper* and led me to think that the way I always defined it needs examining. What is the definition of *prosper*? I always believed that *prosper* had more to do with financial wealth or having all my needs met or enjoying healthy relationships or even just that it should have all been easier. But when I look at Nephi, I realize he went through several things that don't seem prosperous according to my definition. If he was prosperous according to the way I define it, shouldn't he have been successful in getting the brass plates the first time? Shouldn't his brothers have treated him kindly instead of beating him with a rod, binding him with cords, and trying to kill him? If he was prosperous according to my definition, why did Nephi and his family suffer so much for the want of food while journeying in the wilderness? Why did Nephi's bow break?

As I go over these questions, I wonder if I'm just finding evidence for the ways I don't think their journey looked prosperous. After all, I can also find examples of how they prospered according to my definition. They *did* get the records of their fathers. They *were* able to find beasts. They *were* strong and blessed in abundance. The wind drove them toward the promised land.

Then it occurs to me that I need to alter my definition. I don't think that *prosper* means everything is good and easy. I think it describes the journey. I think it's all the things we learn along

---

10. "Mother," Merriam-Webster, https://merriamwebster.com/dictionary/mother (Merriam Webster, 2021).

11. Sheri L. Dew, "Are We Not All Mothers?" *Ensign,* November 2001.

12. "Mothering," Lexico. com, https://www.lexico.com/en/definition/mothering (Oxford University Press, 2021).

the way. It's the lessons that help us grow in our journey back to Heavenly Father and Jesus Christ that make us prosperous. When Nephi's first attempt to get the plates didn't work out, Nephi sought direction from the Lord. He learned that the Lord prepares a way for us to keep His commandments. When Nephi's brothers were mean to him, he learned how to stand for truth and righteousness, forgive, and praise God and not murmur because of his afflictions. He learned to turn to the Lord, believing that the Lord would make known to him answers to the questions he sought.

All those vital lessons do fit the definition of the word *prosperous*. I really do believe that God's work and glory are for all of us to return to Him (see Moses 1:39). Having eternal life feels like prosperity. The Lord knows how to get us there, and His plan includes both the ease of the way and the challenges of the way.

I needed to question my belief that there is a right and a wrong way to think. That questioning helped me discover how my thinking about motherhood and prosperity needed to be modified.

If your current thoughts are not serving you, you want to question them. But how do you go from believing one thing to believing the opposite or a different version of the truth?

When my son participated in high school debate, he found out whether he would argue for the resolution or against it only minutes before the round started. You can argue both for and against your own beliefs. Just look at the opposing view and defend it. There is no harm done. In the end, you get to choose what thought you want to hold on to.

When I adopt a belief, I want to be careful that I like my reasons for doing so. I also need to like the results produced by a specific belief. When I find a belief that fits these criteria, I like to "hold fast that which is good" (1 Thessalonians 5:21).

You know that contradictory beliefs will come for a visit. When they do, you will want to put the pattern for the discovery of truth into practice. You need to either hold fast to your beliefs or put them to the test. Ask the right questions. Will this bring me long-term or short-term pleasure? Do I like the results I am getting? Does this align with who I am?

We all get to believe what we want to believe, which is an important part of our agency. I respect that freedom. Some of my truths come by trial and error. I do not always want to accept that what I am taught is truth. I am grateful we are entrusted individually to "prove all things" (Ibid).

When I was eight years old, I was baptized. Along with the baptism of water came the baptism of fire, receiving the gift of the Holy Ghost. While life experiences can help us discover the truth, so can the companionship of the Holy Ghost. The Holy Ghost is a testifier of truth and is an essential part of obtaining truth.

Are There Absolute Truths?

I believe in absolute truths. They are true even if we don't believe them. You not believing something true does not make it any less true. I'm not an expert on absolute truths, but I'd like to share some of mine:

- Our worth is perfect and unchangeable. Nothing I do or fail to do changes my worth.
- Gravity is a force that attracts matter and pulls it together.
- All human beings are born with agency—the ability to choose.
- All human beings have access to conscience—the ability to decipher right and wrong.
- Humans need connection.

Absolute truths don't vary from one circumstance to another. How you decide to live that truth may vary, but absolute truth itself doesn't. *I crashed into another car and one passenger died* is a circumstance. The absolute truth is *Nothing I do or don't do changes my intrinsic worth. I helped my neighbor with yard work for two months* is a circumstance. The absolute truth is *Nothing I do or don't do changes my intrinsic worth.*

President Spencer W. Kimball shared a letter he wrote to a young man who was looking for truth. In that letter, President Kimball shared the following absolute truths:

God, our Heavenly Father—Elohim—lives.

Jesus Christ is the Son of God, the Almighty, the Creator, the Master of the only true way of life—the gospel of Jesus Christ.

The Gods organized the earth of materials at hand, over which they had control and power.

The Gods organized and gave life to man and placed him on the earth.

Christ mapped out a plan of life for man. . . whereby man might achieve, accomplish, and overcome and perfect himself.

One cannot know God nor understand his works or plans unless he follows the laws which govern.

This Church of Jesus Christ is the only true and living church that is fully recognized with the authority to perform for him, and the only one with a total and comprehensive and true program which will carry men to powers unbelievable and to realms incredible.[13]

I believe The Church of Jesus Christ of Latter-day Saints is Christ's restored church on the earth today. I have believed that for a long time. Should I question that belief? Like many others, I have questioned that at some time in my life while still holding equally fast to it. Why do I continue to believe it? That belief has served me and has been a blessing in my life for fifty-three years. So, I am going to continue to keep it as one of my foundational beliefs.

What do you believe? Take time to figure it out. Like others, you may find that you have contradicting beliefs floating around in your head. Take time to write down your thoughts on paper (see Appendix: Thought Download). That exercise will give you distance from your thoughts and help you examine them individually.

---

13. Spencer W. Kimball, "Absolute Truth," *BYU Speeches*, 6 September 1977.

CHAPTER 4: FEELING

"If we are thinking unwholesome or negative thoughts, it's going to show up in our emotions and eventually our behavior."[1]

—LARRY CRENSHAW, LDS SOCIAL SERVICES

I got out of bed to go to the bathroom in the middle of the night and crumpled to the floor. My head was spinning, and I felt nauseous. I lay very still and imagined all that could be wrong with me. I was finally able to get back to bed, and I managed to carry on with life for a few days until I decided it was time to go to the doctor's office, where I learned I had vertigo. I was given some exercises to correct the condition.

My body experienced physical manifestations—dizziness, nausea, weakness, and fatigue. When we experience physical ailments, our brain goes to work, trying to figure out what we need. The same thing happens when we experience emotional manifestations, such as anxiety and sadness. Our brain thinks, *You shouldn't be feeling this way. What are you going to do about it?* Our brain tries to figure out how to fix the "problem."

Before we talk more about our brain's desire to look for explanations and solutions, let's differentiate between physical and emo-

---

1. Jan Underwood Pinborough, "Keeping Mentally Well," *Ensign*, September 1990.

tional ailments. A physical ailment affects the physical body—a broken bone, a headache, shortness of breath. An emotional ailment originates with a thought that can then create a reaction in the body—worry, fright, excitement. Physical manifestations start in the body and travel to the brain. Emotions occur first in the brain and then travel to the body.

It's helpful to be able to differentiate between the two. Am I feeling tired because I am thinking about all the things I need to get done? That's an emotional manifestation because it starts in the brain with my thinking. Or am I feeling tired because I got only three hours of sleep last night? That's a physical manifestation because it starts in the body. In this chapter, we will discuss the emotional manifestation, or feelings, that start in the brain and move to the body.

Why do feelings matter? Because they are the driving force for everything we do. Let's look at some common examples of actions that were caused by feelings:

- I planned a date night with my spouse because I am invested.
- I saved $5,000 because I was committed.
- I stayed in bed all day because I was depressed.
- I wrote a blog post because I was feeling creative.
- I did nothing on my to-do list because I was tired.
- I snapped at my two-year-old because I was impatient.
- I did not apply for that job because I was feeling inadequate.
- I had a hard conversation because I trusted my parent to listen.

Feelings lead to specific actions. If I am feeling invested in my marriage, my actions are a reflection of that. I schedule date nights. I use kind words. I express gratitude.

If I am committed to saving money, I create a budget and follow it. I do not make impulsive purchases.

Let's look at *faithful* as a feeling. Elder David A. Bednar said, "True faith is focused in and on the Lord Jesus Christ and always leads to righteous action."[2] What kind of actions does the feeling of faithfulness produce?

Ether tells the story of the brother of Jared. We learn that "so great was his faith in God, that when God put forth his finger he could not hide it from the sight of the brother of Jared" (Ether 12:20). Let's break that down into the model:

- **Feeling:** Faithful.
- **Actions:** Cried unto the Lord; followed the Lord's directions: gathered his family and possessions, traveled, and built barges; received chastening; repented; inquired of the Lord; asked the Lord to touch the stones so they would produce light.
- **Result:** The brother of Jared saw Christ.

Feelings drive our actions, which subsequently produce results in our lives. But sometimes we get that backward. We may not take action because we are waiting for the feeling to appear. For example, you might think, *I will prepare my talk for Sunday when the inspiration comes.* Or, *I will run a marathon when I feel motivated.*

Feelings don't just magically appear. We create feelings with our thoughts. The brother of Jared thought, *If I call upon the Lord, "we may receive according to our desires"* (Ether 3:2). That thought created faith, which led to subsequent actions—he called on the Lord, and the Lord touched the stones. Faith is what led the Israelites to walk toward the sea. Faith is what led the priest carrying the ark of the covenant to step into the Jordan River. Faith is what led Noah to build an ark on land. Perhaps you have had this sequence unfold in your own life. Faith is what leads us to kneel in prayer. Faith is what leads us to keep the Sabbath day holy. Faith is why we open our scriptures, take care of the poor and needy, and accept callings.

Our beliefs are what create faith. Faith is what propels our actions. If we want to feel a specific emotion, we would do well to figure out what thoughts create that emotion.

---

2. David A. Bednar, "Ask in Faith," *Ensign*, May 2008.

Let's do that with faith. What thoughts create faith?

Moses initially had thoughts that caused him to doubt his abilities to deliver the Israelites from Egyptian bondage. Eventually, the thought that created faith is reflected in his words, "Let me go" (Exodus 4:18). His faithfulness produced actions that resulted in Israel arriving in the promised land.

If we want to have faith, we can look at the faithful to see what they were thinking.

- I will go and do (1 Nephi 3:7).
- Ask, and it shall be given you (Matthew 7:7).
- Yet will I trust in Him (Job 13:15).
- Behold, *here* I *am* (Genesis 22:1).
- Fear not: for they that *be* with us *are* more than they that *be* with them (2 Kings 6:16).
- So will I go in unto the king (Esther 4:16).
- If I may but touch his garment, I shall be whole (Matthew 9:21).
- Behold the handmaid of the Lord; be it unto me according to thy word (Luke 1:38).
- If thou wilt, thou canst make me clean (Mark 1:40).
- There [is] a just God, and whosoever did not doubt, that they should be preserved by his marvelous power (Alma 57:26).
- Dispute not because ye see not (Ether 12:6).

When you are willing to feel faithful, then you "reap the rewards of your faith" (Alma 32:43). Once we understand that our thoughts create feelings that drive our actions that then produce results, we naturally want to think only positive thoughts so we can feel good all the time. But let's examine the prospect of thinking only positive thoughts.

It's not possible—or even desirable—to feel good all the time. We do not want to feel good about the world's injustices, about severed relationships, or the destruction caused by natural disasters. We do not want to feel happy about a painful health diagnosis or the passing of a loved one. We want and need to have the whole human experience. And having the whole human experience means that we will feel the full range of emotions.

When Heavenly Father presented His plan in the premortal world, "all the sons of God shouted for joy" (Job 38:7). In Doctrine and Covenants 122:7, we learn:

> If thou shouldst be cast into the pit, or into the hands of murderers, and the sentence of death passed upon thee; if thou be cast into the deep; if the billowing surge conspire against thee; if fierce winds become thine enemy; if the heavens gather blackness, and all the elements combine to hedge up the way; and above all, if the very jaws of hell shall gape open the mouth wide after thee, know thou, my son, that all these things shall give thee experience, and shall be for thy good.

We shouted for joy when the plan was presented. We wanted that plan! Why? For the experience. As we just read, all the things we experience are for our good.

We wanted to experience happiness and sadness. Pleasure and pain. Success and failure. Fear and courage. Conflict and assurance. Relaxation and anxiety. Being appreciated and rejected. We could fully understand one emotion only when we had experienced the opposite emotion.

I like to look to Jesus's life as a pattern for how I want to think, feel, and act. Jesus felt a range of emotions. His thoughts about His friend Lazarus dying brought feelings of sadness. His thoughts about the money changers making the temple a den of thieves evoked anger. His thoughts led to frustration when the people were unable to grasp His message, and He said, "O faithless and perverse generation, how long shall I be with you?" (Matthew 17:17). At various times, He also felt compassion, joy, forgiveness, and love. He felt all the emotions we feel, which makes me believe it's okay for us to feel the range of emotions. Why should our life be any different?

Problems occur when we are unwilling to feel all the emotions. When we are unwilling to feel emotions, we push them away. Unfortunately, when we push emotions away, they come back at us in full force.

Imagine that your children have left toys all over the floor. You have asked them to pick the toys up, but they still litter the floor. You feel upset. But you push away the feeling of upset. You tell yourself it's not a big deal. They're just children having fun. These years will not last forever.

Eventually, your children pick up their toys. This occurs for several days. They pretty continually make a mess, but you push the negative feelings away.

That's not all. Your husband cleans up the dinner dishes while you put the kids to bed. When you come back to the kitchen, you notice he did not wipe off the counters or start the dishwasher. You feel upset, but you push that feeling away too.

By the time Saturday comes around, you notice that your kids left a game they were playing earlier in the week on the kitchen table. You come unglued. You start yelling, "Why do I have to do everything around here? Nothing would get done if it wasn't for me!" And there it is: All those feelings you pushed away throughout the week are unleashed at once.

That's just one way we experience our emotions. What are some options for experiencing emotions? You're probably familiar with a few, so let's see how they would play out in the example we just used:

- Push away the emotion. Try to talk yourself into more positive thoughts (which, unfortunately, eventually leads to the upset resurfacing).
- React to the emotion. Just start yelling the first time the kids leave their toys all over the floor. Skip the positive self-talk, and just let everyone know how upset you are that they cannot clean up after themselves.
- Avoid the emotion. Instead of letting the toys on the floor upset you, do something that brings pleasure instead. Shop online. Eat some cookies. Play games on your phone.

As you have probably guessed, none of those options result in long-term benefits. Let's look at one more option for handling emotions: Be willing to feel the emotion. Just feel upset.

Notice the tightness in your chest. Feel the warmth in your torso. Observe the pressure in your head.

When you're willing to feel an emotion, it doesn't last long.

Here's the problem: We don't have much experience with allowing ourselves to feel our emotions. We *do* have experience—usually a lot of it—with fueling our emotions with past grievances, heaping on more negative emotions, and trying to hurry emotions along. Handling emotions by fueling, heaping, and hurrying just increases the longevity of emotions. They seem to stay around longer.

Let me share a personal story of being willing to feel an emotion.

One summer day, my husband was mowing the lawn and I was pulling weeds. He started to loop around the flower bed. There wasn't a bag on the mower, so the grass clippings sprayed on me. I looked at my husband, but he was oblivious. As he looped back around the flower bed, he sprayed me again, still oblivious. The third time he looped around, I jumped up and gave him a dirty look. This time he noticed me and mouthed, "I'm sorry."

I was mad. Instead of feeling it and then letting it go, I fueled my anger with every time in our thirty years of marriage that he hadn't noticed me, that he had been oblivious to me, or that he hadn't cared that he had hurt me. Then I remembered what I had just learned about allowing emotions. I put down my garden tool and went and sat in my hammock. I identified what I was really feeling. It wasn't anger. It was sadness. I was sad that he didn't notice me. When I just allowed myself to feel sad, the feeling lasted less than a minute. In the past, I would have spent the day fuming and thinking about all the past times he hadn't noticed me. Because I was willing to acknowledge that I felt sad when he didn't notice me, I didn't think about it again for the rest of the day.

Be willing to feel your emotions. Feel sad when a parent dies. Feel tired when you have a lot to do. Feel rejected when you don't get invited to a party. Feel regret when you say something you wish you hadn't said.

Another way we make negative feelings bigger is by adding more negative emotions. Let me give you an example. Several years ago, I wrote the script for the Primary presentation. I felt really good about it. When the Primary president read the script, she picked it apart. I felt embarrassed. As time went on, I started to feel annoyed that she had the nerve to ask me to do something and then felt the need to redo it. Then I felt defensive. I had done a good job, and she should have accepted my contribution. Then I felt ashamed that I couldn't do a good enough job in the first place.

If I had been willing to just feel embarrassed—just one emotion—then I probably would have been embarrassed for just a little while and then moved along. But instead of accepting the embarrassment I was feeling, I fed it with many other thoughts that created annoyance, defensiveness, and shame.

Neuroscientist Jill Bolte-Taylor said, "The physiological lifespan of an emotion in the body and brain is 90 seconds."[3] The reason it seems to last longer is that we do not allow it. We do not process it.

Another problem occurs when we attempt to hurry an emotion along. Maybe you've thought something like this:

- You're still sad? That happened ten minutes ago/six months ago/five years ago.
- I don't know why you're excited; that's never going to happen.
- Stop feeling anxious. You're not in danger.
- Don't be jealous. You could have done that if you had tried.

It is okay to feel happy, sad, excited, anxious, and jealous. You don't need to hurry away from those feelings. Feelings are part of the human experience, and you do yourself a disservice when you try to hurry an emotion along.

We also teach our children to hurry emotions along. Have you ever said to your child—or remember your parents saying to you, "You're bored? You'd better not be bored. I will have you scrubbing floors in a hot second." We think our children shouldn't feel bored. We want to give them a chore list a mile long or brainstorm some boredom busters (going on a hike, running to town

---

3. Jill Bolte Taylor, *My Stroke of Insight* (New York: New American Library, 2009).

for ice cream, introducing them to a book series) or come up with a myriad of other ways to try to solve their boredom. When we or our children rush out of our emotions, we don't learn how to process the emotion.

I like to play a game called Spot It with my granddaughter. It is a game of circular cards with pictures on them. When you spot one of your pictures on the draw pile, you get to add it to your pile. Her five-year-old brain is slower than my fifty-three-year-old brain. (I imagine that might change down the road, of course.) Sometimes I say, "Oh, you have the question mark." She then grabs the card I'm referring to and puts it in her pile. That may help her feel good in the short term, but it doesn't help her in the long term. And sometimes I think she is just waiting for me to tell her instead of trying to figure it out for herself.

Similarly, when we try to solve boredom, we just prolong a child's ability to figure out how to process the emotion. We think we are being helpful, and we may be in the short term, but in the big picture, we are interfering with their ability to allow the emotion, let it pass, and move on. Sometimes it seems that children just sit around waiting for us to solve their boredom. But they need to learn how to sit with boredom, and so do we.

What if an emotion is not a problem? Boredom is not a problem. Serenity is not a problem. Embarrassment is not a problem. Shyness is not a problem. Grief is not a problem. Sadness is not a problem. Why do we believe we should be happy all the time? That's an unrealistic expectation in this fallen world. When Adam and Eve were sent forth from the Garden of Eden, both were given the consequence, "I will greatly multiply thy sorrow . . . in sorrow shalt thou eat of it all the days of thy life" (Genesis 3:16-17).

That was only one consequence of the Fall. Another was that we might have joy. "Adam fell that men might be; and men are, that they might have joy" (2 Nephi 2:25). So there we have it. It is our great privilege to feel the full range of emotions. Sorrow *and* joy. The "negative" emotions give us a frame of reference for the "positive" emotions. We would never know the bitter without the sweet—"for if they never should have bitter they could not know the sweet" (D&C 29:39).

There is always going to be a balance. Understanding this helps us go from thinking *this life isn't fair* to thinking *this life is exactly as it is supposed to be.* We move from thinking *why is this happening* to *this is happening for a reason.* The human experience allows for both the ups and the downs. The only reason we can feel the positive emotions is that we know the negative emotions.

If you've decided you are willing to feel an emotion, how do you go about that? First, name the emotion. Then notice how the emotion feels in your body. A feeling is just a vibration. Identify where you are feeling it—in your chest, stomach, behind your eyes. Then allow it to be there. Accept it. Breathe into it.

Sometimes it's easier to explain what a word means by explaining what it *doesn't* mean. Look at how that applies to allowing an emotion:

- Allowing the emotion does not mean judging it. Don't tell yourself that you shouldn't be feeling upset right now.
- Allowing the emotion does not mean having a timeline for it. You don't think, *I wish this sadness would go away right now.*
- Allowing the emotion does not mean reacting to it. You don't slam the door because you are angry.
- Allowing the emotion does mean you're willing to let it be present.

We all experience emotions differently, but the following chart gives some suggestions for how to name an emotion, how to recognize where you feel it in your body, and how to allow the emotion to be present.

NAME IT	NOTICE IT IN YOUR BODY	ALLOW IT
Sad	Droopy shoulders Warmth behind the eyes Heavy heart Weight in stomach	I'm feeling sad, and that is okay.
Fear	Fast heartbeat Paralyzed limbs Hot torso Sweaty Tight chest	Breathe deeply in and out. Relax muscles.
Hopeful	Light heart Weightlessness Shaky heart/excited	Focus on the vibration in your body. Give it all your attention. Notice if the vibration changes.

These techniques for allowing emotions are interchangeable. You can breathe in and out when you are hopeful just as easily as you breathe in and out when you're afraid. You can think, *I am feeling content, and that is okay* just as easily as you can think a similar thing when you are sad. The main thing is just to be present with the vibration in your body. Stay out of your thoughts. You can be aware that your thoughts are coming and going because that is what thoughts do. Just imagine any extra thoughts that try to invade your focus as ocean waves ebbing and flowing. As you practice allowing all the feelings, you will succeed in knowing no feeling is a problem. It is just a vibration in the body.

We tend to make feelings a problem by labeling them as negative or positive. We seek out positive emotions and try to avoid negative ones. We might hope for what Elder Neal A. Maxwell described as expectations for the "Lord, [to] give me experience, but not grief, not sorrow, not pain, not opposition, not betrayal, and certainly not to be forsaken. Keep from me, Lord, all those experiences which made Thee what Thou art! Then let me come and dwell with Thee and fully share Thy joy!"[4]

---

4. Neal A. Maxwell, "Lest Ye Be Wearied and Faint in Your Minds," *Ensign*, May 1991.

We know mortality provides the opportunity to feel all the emotions as we gain the mortal education necessary for growth, so we might want to choose the ones we want to experience. Some of those so-called negative emotions may be worth feeling, including vulnerability, discomfort, contentment, dullness, or peppiness.

Let's look at discomfort as an example. It's not often we hear someone say, "Bring on the discomfort." Unless you are Steven Pressfield, that is. In his book *The War of Art*, he says, "The professional . . . reminds himself it's better to be in the arena, getting stomped by the bull, than to be up in the stands or out in the parking lot."[5] Some people want to embrace the human experience. Some people want to experience the growth that discomfort brings. But for many of us, staying in the comfort zone is the main objective. We think, *Don't put me in a situation where I am going to feel worried, embarrassed, or anxious.* Unfortunately—or maybe fortunately—feeling discomfort is inevitable. We might as well be conscientious about when to feel it.

Why are we willing to feel the discomfort that comes with overeating but not willing to feel the discomfort of hunger? Either way, we are feeling discomfort. Sometimes we avoid pursuing our dreams because it's too uncomfortable. Yet, we also feel discomfort from living below our potential. Be willing to feel the discomfort that comes with pursuing your long-term goals.

Another emotion I have tried to steer clear of is guilt. I decided that guilt was probably a negative emotion and one that I shouldn't feel. But when I searched it out in the scriptures, I discovered it can be an essential emotion that can motivate us to be better.

Let's look at an example of that in the scriptures. Zeezrom was a judge in Ammonihah, and his pocketbook increased or decreased based on the amount of dissension among the people. He constantly stirred up the people, because more contention among them meant more wealth for him. Using his expert skills, he went about questioning Alma and Amulek. It didn't take long for Zeezrom to realize that "Amulek had caught him in his lying and deceiving . . . and

---

5. Steven Pressfield, *The War of Art* (New York: Warner Books, 2002).

seeing that he began to tremble under a consciousness of his guilt" (Alma 12:1). After that, Zeezrom was motivated to be better. He shifted from snaring questions to honest inquiry. He admitted his wrongdoing and became a missionary himself.

Guilt can be an emotion we may choose to feel that can reap positive results if we allow it to move us to positive changes. But please don't confuse guilt with shame. Shame is different from guilt in that it focuses on judging yourself rather than judging your behavior. Shame is an indulgent, unnecessary emotion that keeps us stuck.

Another emotion we sometimes look at as positive is busyness. We focus on finishing task after task to feel productive. We believe the more we get done, the better. Oftentimes what we are doing is just busy work and doesn't even align with our priorities. President Dieter F. Uchtdorf said, "Sad to say, we even wear our busyness as a badge of honor, as though being busy, by itself, was an accomplishment or sign of a superior life."[6] In contrast to our fast-paced life, we have the example of Jesus. He accomplished much, but He took His time to do it. He was never hurried.

The beauty lies in the fact that we get to choose what emotions we want to feel. We are in control of when to feel discomfort, guilt, or busyness. We also get to develop a baseline based on our belief system. For example, being happy is positive, but don't let it cross over to loud laughter or obnoxiousness or to swing in the other direction to contentment or lack of drive. Being vulnerable can invite a special kind of intimacy—being comfortable sharing your feelings. Being vulnerable can also put up a wall—feeling uncomfortable that someone shared their feelings with you. We assign positive or negative connotations based on our belief system. That doesn't make it a truth. Take time to examine your thoughts on specific emotions to see if they are producing the actions you want. Play around with the concept that emotions are not positive or negative. They are just something to be experienced—a vibration in the body that is a signal to us.

---

6. Dieter F. Uchtdorf, "Of Regrets and Resolutions," *Ensign*, November 2012.

Besides labeling emotions as positive or negative, we might look at our definitions of the emotion. I already shared how reevaluating definitions can have an impact. One time, I examined my definition of *self-confidence*. In my mind, self-confidence is a feeling that comes after mastering a skill, because that's when I feel confident. I feel confident that I can put gas in the car. I feel confident that I can brush my teeth well. I have done those things so many times that I feel confident in my ability to do them. To me, if there was a picture in the dictionary for confident people, they would be the ones who walk out on stage and say, "Hello, world! Here I come!" Based on that, I decided I didn't have self-confidence.

But then I read the definition of *self-confidence*: "a feeling of trust in one's abilities, qualities, and judgment."[7] I do trust myself. I have trust in my abilities or my ability to develop qualities I want. I trust my judgment. I trust that whatever is supposed to be happening is happening and that I will be able to handle what comes my way. I have my own back, even through the fails. With that definition, I realized that self-confidence comes from thinking, *I believe in myself.* Self-confidence doesn't necessarily look loud and proud after all like I previously thought. It is just a peaceful assurance. Once I reevaluated based on an accurate definition, I realized I do have self-confidence.

Are you willing to feel all the emotions? Guess what? You don't have to be willing, because it's going to happen anyway. The question really becomes, are you willing to look at emotions as neutral? Are you open to questioning your definition of individual feelings? Are you willing to allow the vibrations in your body? Are you willing to experience emotions as teachers? Are you willing to examine the thoughts that create your emotions and discover the power you possess to feel exactly how you want to feel? And since you can create feelings with your thoughts, are you willing to direct your thoughts so you can be conscious about the emotions you want to experience most of the time?

---

7. "Self-confidence," Lexico.com, https://www.lexico.com/definition/self-confidence (Oxford University Press, 2021).

Pretend you're at a bookstore where there are shelves of emotions (see Appendix: Emotions). If you're trying to be a well-rounded reader in a traditional bookstore, then you choose books from several genres. If you are trying to experience a range of emotions, you choose a variety of emotions.

Be intentional about the emotions you choose. I would rather choose uncomfortable as a feeling over being offended. Why? Being willing to give a talk in church even though I know I am going to feel scared, shy, or uncomfortable will create results in my life—public speaking abilities, increased testimony of the topic I study, and example of overcoming emotions, among them—that help me develop characteristics I want to possess. Feeling offended, on the other hand, will create results in my life that are *not* characteristics I want to develop—things such as strained relationships, avoiding people, and casting blame.

Choose the emotions that will help you get the results you want in life. All the emotions you choose will not be "positive," so make sure you are willing to select a variety. Here's an example:

Paul teaches the Galatian Saints to "not be weary in well doing" (Galatians 6:9). You may choose weary off the shelf of emotions. If you want to feel weary, that's fine, but the good news is that you don't have to choose it. Maybe serving others too much makes you feel weary, while others who serve may feel energized.

Just be intentional about your emotions. Be aware of what you are feeling and notice what you are thinking. Don't compare the emotions you choose to the ones others choose. We are all unique individuals. Ruth may have chosen devotion and willfulness, while Orpah may have chosen comfort and powerlessness.

The emotions we choose will fuel the actions needed to fulfill our individual purpose in life. Consider the emotions chosen by some of those we read about in scriptures.

Deborah felt driven.

Nephi felt inquisitive.

Esther felt brave.

Naaman felt doubtful.

Stephen felt passionate.

Eve felt insightful.

Jonah felt determined.

Martha felt industrious.

It's important to realize that you choose your emotions. They don't just happen to you. Consider these examples:

- He said something offensive, so of course, I am going to feel **offended.**
- No matter how many times I've told her not to slam the door, she still lets it slam. When I hear the door slam, I get **angry.**
- My neighbor brought a plate of cookies, so I inevitably have the **urge** to eat them.
- I am **embarrassed** because I tripped on stage.

We do not feel offended because of something someone says. The door slamming does not make us angry. The cookies do not invite the urge. Tripping is not the cause of our embarrassment. We know the cause of offense, anger, urges, and embarrassment. It is our thoughts:

- He shouldn't have said that.
- I've told her a hundred times not to slam the door.
- Those look delicious.
- What will people think about me?

Circumstances occur—and they don't create your emotions. You have a thought about the circumstance. The thought creates an emotion. You choose your emotions by choosing intentional thoughts.

Once you open up to the idea that you do choose your emotions when you choose your thoughts, then you can look at the world through a whole new lens. Owning your emotions and allowing others to own theirs is called *emotional adulthood*. Emotional adulthood doesn't mean you're above feeling offended, angry, tempted, or embarrassed. You can still be an emotional adult and feel those emotions. (That's one of the joys of living a mortal life.) There are plenty of examples of adults in the scriptures who felt the full range of emotions. Eve had the urge to eat the fruit. Adam and Eve were embarrassed and hid when they heard the Lord's voice. Emotional adulthood is taking ownership of your emotions. Adam and Eve admitted what they had done—"and I did eat" (Genesis 3:12–13).

As an emotional adult, you accept that you chose to be offended. You chose anger as your response. You had an urge. You chose to be embarrassed.

We are not victims of our circumstances. We choose the thoughts we have in response to situations. Both the negative thoughts and the positive thoughts we hear in our brain come from us. We choose the thought we're going to entertain.

Sometimes you may feel overwhelmed by emotions. It seems like a dark cloud enters your being and seems to take over. One of Satan's tools is to use our emotions against us. Satan wants guilt, sadness, and depression to take over and paralyze us. But it doesn't have to be that way. Jesus Christ can deliver us from those overwhelming emotions.

When my dad passed away, my thoughts created feelings of sadness and grief that made me want to crawl back in bed and pull the covers over my head. I did do that. I cried. I allowed the sadness. But because of the Savior, those feelings were replaced with thoughts that evoked hope and optimism.

In another example, my feelings have sometimes been hurt when people have said things to me that invited thoughts of self-loathing. But I don't have to hang on to emotions of self-doubt or victimhood. Instead, I can think about my divine worth—I am a child of Heavenly Parents. I get to choose to feel hated and worthless or loved and worthwhile. Why not enjoy the warm and fuzzy feelings? Why not choose the thoughts that create the feelings I desire?

Jesus Christ has delivered us from unwanted emotions. He knows them. He felt them in the Garden of Gethsemane. I know I will continue to feel emotions; that is just part of this mortal journey. I have felt the deliverance from unwanted emotions that have wanted to darken my world. That deliverance has brought light, hope, and relief. I know the Source to thank for that deliverance.

In the introduction of this book, I talked about needing hands-on tools to help me apply the doctrines of the gospel. Perhaps you know in your heart that Jesus Christ can be your Deliverer, but you need help knowing how to manage overwhelming feelings. Elder Jeffrey R. Holland gave us counsel for those times when he said, "If things continue to be debilitating, seek the advice of reputable people with certified training, professional skills, and good values . . . responsibly consider the counsel they give and the solutions they prescribe."[8]

Our thoughts and feelings make us who we are. Our thoughts and feelings are what we will take into the next life. It will be worth our time and effort here and now to understand the powerful influence our thoughts and feelings have on who we are becoming.

---

8. Jeffrey R. Holland, "Like a Broken Vessel," *Ensign,* November 2013.

CHAPTER 5: ACTIONS

"As soon as you trust yourself, you will
know how to live."

—JOHANN WOLFGANG VON GOETHE

A meditation exercise I did instructed me to repeat "I" on the inhale
and "AM" on the exhale. Then I was instructed to think about my
intentions.

Before we talk about actions that come from our intentions, I
want to focus on I AM. Let's start by looking at the scriptures. I AM
is one of Jesus Christ's names.

- "God said unto Moses, I AM THAT I AM" (Exodus 3:14–15).
- "Listen to the voice of Jesus Christ. . . the Great I Am"
  (D&C 29:1).
- "Be of good cheer, and do not fear, for I the Lord am with
  you, and will stand by you; and ye shall bear record of me,
  even Jesus Christ, that I am the Son of the living God, that
  I was, that I am, and that I am to come" (D&C 68:6).
- When Jesus visited America, He asked His disciples, "What
  manner of men ought ye to be? Verily I say unto you, even
  as I am" (3 Nephi 27:27).

Jesus Christ said I AM before He added:

- The Lamb Slain for You
- The Bread of Life

- The Source of Living Water
- Your Healer[1]

Similarly, all of us ARE before we add any actions to our list. Consider some of the labels used to define us.

- I am a college graduate.
- I am a foodie.
- I am a millionaire.
- I am a high school dropout.
- I am divorced.
- I am a world traveler.
- I am a cancer patient.
- I am short.
- I am American.
- I am insecure.

Before I address the impact our actions have on the results we create in our lives, I want to talk about our worth. We are born worthy. I think we get in our mind that the more we do—the more positive action we take—the more worthy we are. But that is simply not true.

We are worthy because we are. Nothing we do or don't do changes our worth. A $100 bill is worth $100 whether it is fresh off the printing press or is torn, dirty, and crinkled.

We get so busy doing things—taking dinner to a sick neighbor, driving the kids to play practice, volunteering at the food bank, enrolling in educational classes, accepting callings, taking care of ailing parents, cleaning and organizing our homes, calling a friend. In all the doing, we become frazzled and spread thin.

Taking action can be a good thing, but we want to examine our reasons for doing something. When we understand that our doing comes from a place of "I am a good person," we don't feel the need to do more than is necessary. In that case, doing things

---

1. Stephen P. Schank, "I Am That I Am: Symbols of Jesus Christ in the Old Testament," *Ensign*, December 2018.

comes from a place of love and wanting to fulfill our potential. When we can act from a place of worthiness, we are not doing things because we want the accolades, the recognition, or the respect of others. We act from a place of "I want to," not a place of "I should" or "I shouldn't have."

Sometimes we engage in actions that take us down a road we did not want to go down. We yell at our children, speed down the freeway, neglect family, overspend, gossip, read or watch inappropriate content, tell a lie, disrespect an employee. The list goes on. Life and our choices tend to knock us around, but they do not change our worth. Regretful choices do not define us, either. What we do or do not do does not define our worth. We are divine children of God. We are much more than what we are doing.

In junior high, I had an assignment to compile a book of poetry. The only lines I still remember came from an Emily Dickinson poem that resonated with me and said, "I'm Nobody! Who are you? Are you—Nobody—too?" Leave it to the middle school years to teach that everything I have or haven't done up to that point has defined me as an athlete, a nerd, a cool kid, or none of the above. Of course, those are just thoughts I chose to believe and accept as truth until I chose to accept new truths. One of those new truths says that even though I am torn and dirty and crinkled, I am still "worth worlds."[2]

How worth it am I—are all of us? Jesus Christ gave His life for me and for you. He willingly chose to be crucified. He fulfilled the atoning sacrifice that provides salvation for every one of us. He did this even before I stumbled over personal trials and entertained temptations. He knew we would make less than stellar decisions in mortality. Even with that knowledge, He knew we were worth saving. I AM worth it to Him before mortality, during mortality, and after mortality. I AM His work and His glory. When I look in the mirror or at another human being, I want to see the worth He sees. Because it is 100 percent there. He loves us, and we can love

---

2. Brigham Young, "Remarks," *Deseret News,* March 6, 1861, 2.

ourselves. We can love the good within us, the bad within us, and the ugly within us too.

If you are still struggling with believing your worth, go back to the thought chapter and write down some of your beliefs. Question them. Take them through the process to determine if they are serving you. Otherwise, move on to the question, "If we are worth worlds already, why do anything? Why not just sit on the couch watching television and eating bonbons?"

President Gordon B. Hinckley said, "We have a great work to do. Every [teacher, officer, father, mother, husband, wife, child] can be better than he or she is today. We are on the road that leads to immortality and eternal life and today is part of it."[3]

We can be better, but why take any actions if taking action doesn't change our worth? Because we have the potential. We take action for the growth it brings.

Philippians 2:12 tells us, "Work out your own salvation." Sometimes I think I would love salvation to be given to me, wrapped up in a nice little package with a bow on top. But would I really? There is something extremely satisfying about putting in the work and enjoying the rewards of that work. As challenging as it can be sometimes, I am very grateful for the agency part of God's plan. The ability to act and not be acted upon. As we exercise our agency to act, we are becoming the best version of ourselves. We use our gifts and talents to fulfill our purpose. We use our strengths and weaknesses to traverse our mortal experience.

Looking to Jesus's mortal experience helps me pause, ponder, and evaluate what I want my experience to look like. It is important to remember how much He does love us and is aware of how we are trying to be the best version of ourselves. I believe His counsel is a gift and not something He would want us to use as a shaming tool. We are already worthy because He already gave us the greatest gift—even before we came to earth and made unfortunate choices. I think He just wants us to know as much

<hr />

3. Gordon B. Hinckley, "Messages of inspiration from President Hinckley," *Church News*, November 4, 1995.

as possible so that when the future comes we will be at peace with where we stand.

You're probably familiar with word clouds—images made of words. The words that are more important or that are frequently used appear in a much larger text. Imagine recording everything you do in a week and entering that information in a word cloud generator. What words would be in the largest text? The smallest? With so many options of things we can do, it's smart to take inventory of what we're doing to make sure our actions are aligned with our purpose.

Deciding on our purpose and the actions to take is unique to each individual. Let's look at some examples.

INDIVIDUAL	IDENTIFIED PURPOSE	ACTION
Emma D&C 25	Comfort to Joseph Smith	• Used consoling words • Acted as scribe • Expounded scriptures • Exhorted the Church • Learned much
Lehi 1 Nephi 1	Prophesy	• Told the people what he had seen and heard
Rahab Joshua 2, 6	Deliver her family	• Hid two spies •Proposed oath of safety • Assisted spies out of the city • Bound scarlet thread in the window • Gathered her family
Deborah Judges 4–5	Prophetess	• Judged Israel • Offered her counsel • Accompanied Barak • Prophesied • Praised the Lord
Joseph Smith Joseph Smith–History	Restore Jesus Christ's Church	• Translated and published The Book of Mormon • Received revelation • Received priesthood authority and ordained others • Restored ordinances and principles • Organized the Church • Sent missionaries out • Directed the building of temples

We want to take actions that align with our purpose. Of course, sometimes we choose to act in ways that are not the best version of ourselves.

Remember that our time on earth is an opportunity to gain experience. We're supposed to mess up and do dumb things. When a baby is learning to walk, we don't berate him when he falls. We encourage him. That is what we can do for ourselves. We can cheer ourselves on when we don't show up as our best selves, then we can get up and try again.

Philippians 3:13 says, "But this one thing I do, forgetting those things which are behind, and reaching forth unto those things which are before." I love that Paul could forget and forgive himself for the things he did as Saul. We all have a past. We all have done things we wish we hadn't done. We can leave those things behind and move forward reaching for the good.

The important thing as we move through mortality is to learn as much as we can, and that happens even when we do something poorly. Not showing up as our best provides a great opportunity to learn how to do it better next time. As examples of that, let's look at some people from the scriptures to determine what they did and what they learned.

Sariah complained. She also learned with a surety that their trip into the wilderness had a purpose and that the Lord protected her sons (see 1 Nephi 5:2, 8).

Joseph Smith "fell into many foolish errors" (JS—H 1:28). He learned that God forgives our "sins and follies" and is willing to give us a "manifestation . . . of [our] state and standing before him" (JS—H 1:29).

The Israelites continually made blunders on their trip to the promised land. They murmured, failed to follow the prophet's counsel, did not keep their covenants, and worshipped idols, just to name a few of their errors. They learned that our personal journeys can be long. It took forty years to travel a journey that should have taken "eleven days" (Deuteronomy 1:2). They also learned the Lord keeps His promises.

We do not succeed or fail. We succeed or learn.

We complain. We make foolish errors. We choose the hard way. We learn. President Russell M. Nelson said, "Our spirits rejoice with every small step forward we take."[4] Some of those steps make the strait and narrow path curvy. But with the effort, we are learning and growing.

There's a caveat: We learn and grow only if we are making choices. Sometimes we get paralyzed by indecision. At times, we are afraid to act because we are afraid of making the wrong decision. President Spencer W. Kimball said, "Indecision and discouragement are climates in which the Adversary lives to function, for he can inflict so many casualties among mankind in those settings. . . . If you have not done so yet, decide to decide!"[5]

We want to make sure we buy the perfect house, take the perfect job, say the perfect thing, raise the perfect children. When Jesus invited us to "be perfect even as I, or your Father who is in heaven is perfect," He had already been resurrected (3 Nephi 12:48). That takes the pressure off of being perfect now. But we can definitely be making progress toward perfection. Why? Because we can. Because we are capable. Because it feels good. Perfection is defined as "something in a constant state of evolution or change."[6] President Nelson shares that "*perfect* was translated from the Greek *teleios* which means 'complete.'"[7] He says, "Please note that the word does not imply 'freedom from error'; it implies 'achieving a distant objective.'" There you have it. Let that resonate with you. Perfect does not mean never making mistakes. All those twists and turns make for a perfectly beautiful life. The purpose of life is to *live* and *learn*.

Recently my thoughts held a conversation about my future. I feel like I devoted my life to raising my children. And it was totally worth it! They are such amazing adults. Now, as I look to my future, I think of things I would like to pursue: being employed as a life

---

4. Russell M. Nelson, "Welcome Message," *Ensign,* May 2021.
5. Spencer W. Kimball, "Boys Need Heroes Close By," *Ensign,* May 1976, 46.
6. "Perfection," *Urbandictionary.com,* https://www.urbandictionary.com/define.php?term=Perfection (Urban Dictionary, 2021).
7. Russell M. Nelson, "Perfection Pending," *Ensign,* November 1995.

coach, volunteering in my community, writing, and serving a mission, among others. But I also still want to be there for my children and grandchildren. Do I want to focus my time on being available to my children and grandchildren, or do I want to pursue personal growth? I don't know if I have the time and energy to do all the things I'd like to do.

As I mulled over these thoughts, the parable of Mary and Martha came to mind. All of my intended pursuits are good, just like both Mary and Martha's pursuits were good: serving the Lord and learning from the Lord. The problem came when Martha wanted the Lord to tell Mary to choose something different. I concluded that "it mattereth not" (D&C 80:3) to the Lord what I choose—focusing on my family or focusing on personal growth—as long as I am happy with the decision and am not judging people who chose differently from me and I am not having regrets.

That's not all. By choosing one, I'm not negating the other. I don't have to choose whether to focus on my family *or* focus on personal growth. I can do both. Different times in our lives call for different priorities. Ecclesiastes 3:1 teaches, "To every thing there is a season, and a time to every purpose under the heaven." Sometimes you might think that you're not balancing your actions well because you're giving a disproportionate amount of time to your profession or to your calling or to your family. When that happens, it can help to look at your life as a whole. Sometimes certain things in your life really do require more attention; look for balance over a lifetime, not just during a week or even a year.

Realize, too, that things of great value often take more time than we would originally think. When I get in a hurry to accomplish something, I remind myself of how important it was for the Book of Mormon to roll forth. Yet *four years* passed from the time Moroni appeared to Joseph Smith until Joseph received the plates. It took another *three years* for them to be published. Regardless of how long something takes, the important thing is how we are developing our character, what we are learning, and how we are handling our experiences. And those things happen as we "press forward to and through the proving, examining, and trying experiences of [our] lives."[8]

As we press forward, we have the opportunity to make innumerable decisions. We also get to own the outcomes of those decisions. I may decide to eat too much at Thanksgiving dinner. I decide to put all the food in my mouth, and with that decision comes lethargy, discomfort, and weight gain. I may decide to go on a walk with a friend, and with that decision comes exercise, companionship, and fresh air. I may decide to take a new job, with an outcome of more money, uncomfortable adjustments, and new skills. Whenever you make a decision, you need to expect the outcome of that decision.

Another thing to consider with each action is the feeling that drives it. Here's what I mean: Moroni 7:6–7 says, "God hath said a man being evil cannot do that which is good; for if he offereth a gift, or prayeth unto God, except he shall do it with real intent it profiteth him nothing. For behold, it is not counted unto him for righteousness."

The invitation at the end of the Book of Mormon reinforces that the feelings driving our actions makes a difference. In Moroni 10:4, we read that we should ask "with a sincere heart, with real intent, having faith in Christ." When we ask with these feelings at our core, then we will achieve the result—a manifestation of the truth we are seeking.

Let's look at how the feeling of "intent" is manifest in two different examples.

In the first example, when Joseph Smith went into a grove of trees to pray, his intent came from a sincere desire to know which church he should join. He might have had a completely different experience if the feeling driving his action had been skepticism, arrogance, or belligerence. In the second example, the Zoramites' prayers on the Rameumptom came from pride. They said, "We believe that thou hast elected us to be thy holy children; and also thou hast made it known unto us that there shall be no Christ" (Alma 31:16).

Let's see how those two examples look when put into the model. As you can see, the action was the same—but because of the feelings underlying the action, the results were completely different.

---

8. David A. Bednar, "We Will Prove Them Herewith," *Ensign*, November 2020.

Joseph Smith's Prayer

- **C:** Prayer.
- **T:** I seek communication with God through prayer.
- **F:** Sincerity.
- **A:** I go somewhere private, pray, and ask a question.
- **R:** I receive a manifestation of truth.

Zoramites' Prayer

- **C:** Prayer.
- **T:** I seek to tell God what a "chosen and a holy" person I am (Alma 31:18).
- **F:** Pride.
- **A:** Build a tower, pray, and boast.
- **R:** I receive a manifestation of self.

This is another opportunity to use the model as a tool to bring awareness. We have been commanded to pray. So we pray. What is the problem? There is no problem. There is only awareness.

After applying the action to the model, you can start asking the questions.

Why do I pray?

Do my prayers sound different when I'm praying by myself than they do when I'm praying with others? Why?

Do I like my result?

Would I rather find the truth or be right?

The answers to your questions will help you know where to go from here. They will also help you determine which components of the model need tweaking.

The feeling component of the model is critical. Sometimes results are starkly different even though the models are exactly the same except for the feeling driving the action. Let me share an example.

While I was serving as an online seminary teacher, I noted that the two enrolled students were not doing their work. When no one showed up to the video conference call after the first week,

I reached out to the parents. One of the parents said, "He just doesn't have time."

My first thought was to send my student the object lesson of rocks in a jar. The object lesson is a visual demonstration that teaches if we do the important things first, we will have time for the little things. Sand, pebbles, rocks, and water represent the things we would like to accomplish in a day. The rocks hold the highest priority—perhaps reading scriptures, praying, and spending time with family. The pebbles, sand, and water also represent things we'd like to accomplish during the day that don't hold the same weight of importance—things like reading a book, watching a movie, or washing dishes. If we put the rocks into the jar first, there is enough room for the smaller things to go in; they filter down in between the rocks. But if we put the small things in the jar first, there is no room for the rocks.

I did a model on what I was thinking and feeling. It looked like this:

- **Circumstance:** Mom said, "He just doesn't have time."
- **Thought:** He needs that object lesson.
- **Feeling:** Prideful.
- **Action:** Mail the letter.
- **Result:** I know what's best for my student.

I didn't send the object lesson to my student then, even though I thought he needed it. About a week later, I thought, *I should send him that object lesson. It might help.* This time I was coming from a place of love, and my model looked like this:

- **Circumstance:** Mom said, "He just doesn't have time."
- **Thought:** He needs that object lesson.
- **Feeling:** Love.
- **Action:** Mail the letter.
- **Result:** I offer help.

My thought and action were the same in both models. But the *feeling* that prompted the action was very different. Does it really matter if the feeling is different if we are taking the same action? The reason I didn't send the object lesson while feeling prideful was that I don't want the result in my life of thinking I know what's best for others. I do want to be the kind of person whose results come from a place of love and a desire to offer help.

The same feeling can also drive different actions. The Anti-Nephi-Lehis buried their weapons of war as a testimony and covenant to God. On the other hand, Moroni rallied the troops to fight. Two groups of people believed in God, believed they were doing God's will and were willing to die rather than transgress or forsake their God. Let's look at their models.

Anti-Nephi-Lehi Model

- **C:** War.
- **T:** "If our brethren destroy us, behold, we shall go to our God and shall be saved" (Alma 24:16).
- **F:** Conviction.
- **A:** Bury my weapons of war.
- **R:** Salvation of his people.

Moroni Model

- **C:** War
- **T:** "We covenant with our God, that we shall be destroyed . . . if we shall fall into transgression" (Alma 46:22).
- **F:** Conviction.
- **A:** Fight for God, religion, freedom, peace, wives, and children.
- **R:** Redeemed by the Lord.

Sometimes we believe the strait and narrow path looks the same for all of us. These models demonstrate the error in that thinking. The covenants of both groups were their straight and narrow path. The actions they took looked vastly different.

Our actions matter because they produce the results in our lives. Many apostolic talks have described the blessings the Lord wants to pour out on us. And while some blessings may come as a gift—such as sunshine bursting out from behind clouds, a hot meal, or medical care—there was definitely some action taken to produce those results. We enjoy the result of sunshine, but it took a creative period to be organized: "God said, Let there be light: and there was light" (Genesis 1:3). We enjoy a hot meal the neighbor drops off, but she put in the effort to shop, combine the ingredients, and deliver it. We may enjoy an antibiotic to destroy disease in our bodies, but behind the medicine is years of research, laboratory work, and diagnostic education. All results depend on action.

In John 1:39, Jesus invites His disciples to "come and see." I love the "come and see" part of life. What are other people doing? How is it working for them? I love reading self-help books. There was a period in my life when I picked up one after another, and I often felt like a better person having just read the book. At some point, I realized it was not doing me any good if I just kept reading and didn't pause in my learning and translate that knowledge into action.

We need to realize, too, that our action needs to be purposeful and intentional. William H. Bennett said, "Action is all-important, but action alone is not enough."[9] Coming and seeing is not enough. If we want to bring forth fruits, then we need to not just take action, but "the right kind of action, purposeful action—the things we do should add up in meaningful ways and contribute to rich, purposeful living here and bring eternal joy hereafter."[10]

Jesus Christ did not just tell us to get baptized; He got baptized. Jesus invites us to engage. We see evidence of that invitation throughout scripture; the following are just a few examples:

"Lift up the hands which hang down, and strengthen the feeble knees" (D&C 81:5).

"Let us run with patience the race that is set before us" (Hebrews 12:1).

---

9. William H. Bennett, "Inertia," *Ensign*, May 1974.
10. Bennett.

"Do good; let earth and hell combine against you" (D&C 6:34).

"Men should be anxiously engaged in a good cause, and do many things of their own free will, and bring to pass much righteousness" (D&C 58:27).

President Nelson said, "His gospel provides an invitation to keep changing, growing, and becoming more pure."[11] I remember a time when general conference depressed me. During that time, I thought, *There is so much I should be doing.* That thought brought feelings of overwhelm and discouragement. At some point, I had a change of heart, though, and started to feel excited that God believed I could become that person. Now instead of feeling guilty, I feel excited that God believes I have that much potential.

Take the actions necessary to reach your full potential. If you want to enhance your life, make plans for where you want to go and what you need to do to get there. *Preach My Gospel* specifies, "Goals reflect the desires of our hearts and our vision of what we can accomplish. Through goals and plans, our hopes are transformed into action. Goal setting and planning are acts of faith."[12] Start taking the actions necessary to create the life you want. As you take those first steps, you are on the path to fulfilling the measure of your creation. As Elder Dieter F. Uchtdorf said, God "will illuminate the path ahead and open our eyes to see our unknown and perhaps unimagined talents."[13]

During a time in my life when I was passively devouring self-help literature, I decided to take the personality trait quiz offered in the book I was reading. The quiz summary informed me that one of my characteristics was a lack of motivation. It went on to say that I was not a goal setter. I took issue because I love setting goals. A few days later, I stumbled across a goal list I'd made a few years earlier and realized I was great at goal setting—I just never took action to accomplish the goals (which is what the book really meant).

11. Russell M. Nelson, "Welcome Message."
12. *Preach My Gospel: A Guide to Missionary Service* (Salt Lake City, UT: The Church of Jesus Christ of Latter-day Saints, 2004), 146.
13. Dieter F. Uchtdorf, "Of Regrets and Resolutions," *Ensign,* November 2012.

Out of pride or determination or spite or some personality trait that probably didn't even belong to my designated color, I decided to prove that book wrong. One of the goals on the list I found was to run a half-marathon. I loudly proclaimed, "I will show you, book!" I started training and ran my first half-marathon within the year. Since then, I have been a successful goal-setter and a successful goal-accomplisher. I am a believer that goals are vital tools in helping us achieve our purpose.

Let's analyze the experience I had around deciding to run that half-marathon. Once I decided the result I wanted—to run a half-marathon—I needed a plan of action. I found a step-by-step running schedule online and started following it. I bought some running shoes. I carved out time in my day. Breaking goals down into simple steps and following through does equate to big results.

As I was trying to run that first practice mile without stopping, I was not thinking about the 13.1 miles I would have to run in the half-marathon. I was trying to run only one mile. Each effort made a difference. Seems simple, right? The great thing about taking action is that it is accompanied by the other components of the model.

Of course, my thoughts wanted to get in on the action. Here are some of the ones that ran through my head as I was training:

I don't want to do this.

What was I thinking?

Ugh, I'm losing a toenail. Maybe I shouldn't run today.

My emotions wanted to be felt, too. I felt scared. Doubtful. Discouraged.

It is during this action phase that a lot of our growth takes place. If we want the result, then we have to do the thought work and be willing to feel our emotions as we take action. We have to make a plan for the obstacles that will surface because they will surface. Don't be surprised. Anticipate as many obstacles as you can and make strategies for each of them. If new obstacles arise, create new strategies.

Let me share one of the obstacles I faced as I prepared to run my second half-marathon. When thoughts surfaced about not wanting to train that day, I did thought work. I remembered my reasons for doing it. This time it was not to spite the personality quiz; it was for the example I was setting for my children. I wanted them to know that taking time for personal achievements is a worthy pursuit. It was for my health and well-being. It was for the enjoyment running brought me. When emotions like lack of motivation, apathy, and fatigue surfaced, I allowed them to be there and followed through on my commitment anyway. I focused on the long-term result, not the short-term pleasures.

President Dallin H. Oaks said, "Take the long view. What is the effect on our future of the decisions we make in the present?"[14] I realized I needed to make decisions with the long-term goal in focus.

Other obstacles cropped up as I was training for that second half-marathon. The biggest obstacle came the week before the entry deadline for the race. The local newspaper published an article about the race sponsor, and I decided I didn't want my entry fee supporting their business. I searched for another race nearby that coincided with my availability, but I couldn't find one. I was determined to run, so I went to Plan B. I charted my own course, put on my running shoes, and achieved the result I had worked for.

Don't let obstacles derail you from your goals. Recognize them for what they are and make new strategies to help you overcome them. One January I made a goal to save a specific amount of money that year. I broke down how much I needed to save each month and how I was going to do it. By the end of January, I didn't have the money I had planned to put into savings that month. As a matter of fact, some unexpected expenses brought the dollar amount of my savings account lower than what I began with. I decided my savings plan was not going to happen and I might as well table that goal. And that's what I did.

Too often we give up on goals before we even give them a chance. Expect obstacles, but stay focused. You may even have to change your target date for completion, but you will get a whole lot closer to achieving your goal if you keep trying than if you give up completely.

---

14. Dallin H. Oaks, "Where Will This Lead," *Ensign*, May 2019, 60–61.

As you set goals and take the necessary actions, you will start to believe that there is nothing you can't do if you set your mind to it. You will live in integrity with yourself, and that's a pretty enjoyable place to be.

CHAPTER 6: RESULT

"You may never know what results come from your action. But if you do nothing, there will be no result."

—MOHANDAS KARAMCHAND GANDHI

When my daughter was in junior high, her friends were convinced that she was not Christian. They didn't conclude that from observing her actions, because she was a sweet, friendly, charitable young woman. Their conclusion came from statements they had heard from others about our religion.

She testified of her beliefs to her friends as best she could, but I eventually felt a need to write those friends and their families a letter. In the letter, I included the scripture, "By their fruits ye shall know them" (Matthew 7:20). We were doing our best as a family to walk the Christian road of discipleship, and I hoped they would know my daughter was Christian by who she was trying to be.

The tending of the tree—the pruning, the digging, the nourishing—are the actions we take. We may classify our actions as good or bad, and we may expect our results to reflect that. Good actions equal good results and bad actions equal bad results, right? No—that's not always the case.

Consider these examples:

- Took out the trash. Good or bad?
- Didn't reach out to my ministering families in June. Good or bad?

- Watched television on Sunday. Good or bad?
- Took cookies to the neighbors. Good or bad?

The answers to those may seem simple, but they don't take into account the numerous factors connected to the doing. Let's look a little deeper: You took out the trash after someone asked you to twenty times. Good or bad? You didn't reach out to your ministering families in June because your son was hospitalized with a serious illness. Good or bad?

Not quite as easy that time, was it?

Our thoughts, feelings, and actions all play into the results we are creating—who we are becoming. Are our fruits good, or bad, or do they just need more attention? All the tending and pruning did not guarantee good fruit. Likewise, our intentional actions do not always guarantee the results we are striving for. They do guarantee results, though, and we can glean knowledge from those results. Remember learning to regard circumstances as neutral? You can do the same thing with results. Instead of looking at them as good results or bad results, you can just treat them as information.

Let's say you want to save $5,000. You decide on several actions that will help you achieve that result: Take a break from online shopping. Get a part-time job. Walk to the store. Cancel the cable.

You do all those things, but your savings account doesn't show that result. You weren't able to save $5,000. Why? Other factors entered the scenario. The car needed a new transmission. The heating bill was higher this month. You took a sick day.

When our actions do not equate to the results we hoped for, the right thing to do is to examine the model and use what we learn to make needed changes. The *wrong* thing to do is to follow our probable first reaction: to throw in the towel. We think, *I didn't achieve the result I wanted, so I guess it isn't meant to be.* We condemn ourselves. We think, *I knew I was not going to be able to do that.* We give up on the result (and ourselves) rather than using the information to alter what is in our control.

Maybe we just need to do something as simple as extending the deadline. Not achieving our desired results on our timeline is not a problem. Ecclesiastes 9:11 teaches, "The race is not to the swift, nor the battle to the strong."

Let me share an example from my own life. Recently I over-hydrated, and my sodium levels became low. I sweated out the electrolytes my body needed. I went from over-hydrating and not salting my food to under-hydrating and salting everything in an attempt to get my numbers in the right range. I was in a hurry to feel "normal" again. It didn't work. My body had to readjust on its own timetable.

We don't need to be in a hurry to create results. Everything is happening at the perfect pace. Too often we get discouraged when we don't accomplish things at the pace we planned for. Or we compare ourselves to others and their pace instead of focusing on our own lives. We need to focus only on the results we are creating. Does the deadline we set for our result really matter? What matters is that we are still working toward it.

President Thomas S. Monson said, "Our task is to become our best selves. One of God's greatest gifts to us is the joy of trying again, for no failure ever need be final."[1] If the result is really something to be desired, keep going back to the vineyard. Keep taking action until you get the result you want. Recalculate.

Try changing your thoughts about what's happening. Instead of thinking, *I'm never going to be able to save that much*, or, *Something always happens that prevents me from saving*, think, *I'm one step closer to $5,000*, or, *I'm learning how to handle unforeseen circumstances*. Many thoughts are available to you. Which ones will help you move forward?

Maybe you can change your feelings about what's happening. Instead of feeling discouraged or angry, you could feel challenged or curious. There are so many feelings available. Which feelings are going to help you reach your goals?

Maybe some different actions need to occur. Going back to that

---

1. Thomas S. Monson, "The Will Within," *Ensign*, May 1987.

goal of saving $5,000, maybe you could carpool, ask for a raise, have a garage sale, or cancel your monthly subscriptions. All is not lost. Although your original plan didn't work out, there are always other options.

A group of people we are all familiar with had a goal: get to the promised land. The result they wanted was to possess "from the wilderness and this Lebanon even unto the great river, the river Euphrates, all the land of the Hittites, and unto the great sea toward the going down of the sun, shall be your coast" (Joshua 1:4).

We all have innumerable models throughout our lifetime, and the Israelites were no different. Let's focus on a mashed-up model with this result in mind.

- **R:** The promised land.
- **A:** Murmured, battled, rebelled, doubted, repented, pressed forward, rested, forgot, remembered.
- **F:** Fear/bravery.

They vacillated between fear and bravery, obedience and rebellion, doubt and resolve. Sound familiar? That's what happens to each of us on the road to getting the results we want. We are human, and the human experience includes opposition. The thing to remember is that the results we desire are out there. There may be obstacles, and they may not come on our timetable. But they are achievable if we stay focused on taking the next best action. And even if our results are not achieved in this life—like they weren't for Moses—we will be better for the experience, just like he was.

Results are not the actions we take. Results are the consequences of our actions. And those consequences can teach us. Elder Taniela B. Wakolo said, "I will no longer refer to my challenges as trials and tribulations but as my learning experiences."[2] We can look at results that didn't turn out as we wanted as a punishment or as a treasure trove of knowledge. All those speed

---

2. Taniela B. Wakolo, "God Loves His Children," *Ensign,* May 2021.

bumps along the way are just an opportunity for us to grow and to find out what we are made of. Will we reevaluate? Will we press forward? Or will we give up?

On December 30, 2017, our home burned. It was classified as a total loss. The insurance company came through for us, and the result is a beautiful home. Getting there was painful and messy and taxing. Any time we work toward a desired result, it can be painful and messy and taxing—but the result is generally so worth it. Getting a beautiful home was not my only result.

I learned patience.

It reinforced my knowledge that my adult children are the most amazing people in the world.

I learned how to receive gratefully.

I was touched by the kindness of strangers.

I acquired new carpentry skills.

My support group exceeded my expectations.

I recognized so many tender mercies.

I was reminded that God knows me and knows how to help me grow into the person He sees.

I found that loved ones on the other side of the veil can send messages.

I developed increased compassion and love for others in their trials.

I developed design and style talents.

I learned things along the way. My character was stretched. I "increased in wisdom and stature" (Luke 2:52). The learning was priceless.

This week I have been thinking about goals I have set, results I want, and the person I am becoming along the way. Sure, reaching my goal weight would be amazing. But the reward really comes from the internal discipline, integrity, and focus I achieve in the process. The rewards come long before the result of the number on the scale. The rewards come as my body gets stronger as I work out. The rewards come as my medical numbers (blood pressure, body mass, and blood sugar levels) get in a healthy range. The rewards come as I let go of unwanted habits and adopt wanted ones. The rewards come as I allow urges and desires for certain foods but do not act on those emotions. The rewards come as I love and support myself even when I eat something unplanned. While I may not see the end result fast enough, I am celebrating the smaller results along the way.

We may never see our desired result. Some couples yearn for children, but they never come. Some long to be out of debt, but there is never enough money. Some may never find a job in the line of work they were educated for. Even when the results we work so hard for never come, we can rest assured that things are happening exactly as they were meant to happen.

Sister Michelle Craig shared a message from Elder Jeffrey R. Holland: "Reflecting on his life, his greatest growth has come from disappointment or unfulfilled expectations."[3] Maybe this was also the case for Mormon, who was after a specific result—to defeat the Lamanites. Let's take a look at his model.

- **R:** Defeat the Lamanites.
- **A:** Led the Nephite army, defended the city, prepared for war, fortified the city.

Mormon took action toward his goal, yet it was not realized. As he put it, "Notwithstanding all our fortifications, the Lamanites did . . . drive us out of the city" (Mormon 2:4). Even though Mormon took significant measures to reach his goal, he did not succeed.

The same thing will happen for us. What about the couple who wants children? Their actions toward that result may include physical intimacy, taking the wife's temperature, tracking her cycle, and seeing a specialist. Still, the result of children may not happen.

Some much-desired-for results will not come no matter how much action we take. So why even try? Why set goals if they may

---

3. Gospel Library App., Audiences, Women, "Sister to Sister Event," *2021 BYU Women's Conference*, 39:10.

never be realized? Why put in all the work and never enjoy the rewards?

Why? Because the result is not always the reward. There are so many incremental rewards along the way. Increased understanding. Empathy for others. Newly developed characteristics.

When the desired result is not occurring, you may decide it is time to shift gears. You may decide it is time to pursue something else. That doesn't mean you're giving up. It doesn't mean you're quitting. It doesn't equate to failure. It means you are making a conscious decision to pursue new goals.

On the other hand, if you are not ready to end the pursuit of the goal, you may need to examine if there is anything that can be done differently. Go back to the drawing board. Look at the model—circumstance, thought, feeling, and actions. Each component impacts the results. Evaluate and experiment as needed. Then make a decision and move in that direction so you can gain more knowledge.

When I studied Ether in the Book of Mormon, I wondered why building a tower to heaven failed. It seems like a great idea. Who wouldn't want to do that? For answers, let's look at the model.

- **Circumstance:** Tower of Babel.
- **Thought:** "Let us build us a city and a tower, whose top *may reach* unto heaven" (Genesis 11:4).
- **Feeling:** Rebellious, defiant. (Ether doesn't tell us about the feeling driving the action. But Rabbinical literature indicates the intent of the builders was to engage in war with God.
- **Actions:** Made brick, used slime for mortar, spoke ill of God.
- **Result:** Language was confounded, people were scattered.

The feeling line might be the most important component to examine. If they wanted to reach heaven and approached that goal with humility instead of defiance, they might have reached heaven in a burning bush or on the top of a mountain or through a still, small voice. No need to point out the mote in our brother's eye, though, when we have a beam in our own.

Let me share an all-too-familiar scenario in the average household.

- **C:** Husband said, "You idiots! Can't you keep your Legos off the floor?"
- **T:** He shouldn't yell at the kids.
- **F:** Anger.
- **A:** I yell at my husband.
- **R:** I do the exact behavior I was condemning.

We think our thought is truth, but the feeling component trips us up from getting the result we want. Those feelings lead to actions that are not going to help us get the results we want. Let's take a look at our thoughts and how they play into the specific scenario of a trial. (Just fill in the blank here; for our purposes, any trial will do.) Notice how our thought trickles down to our feelings and actions and gives us an individualized result.

- **C:** Trial.
- **T:** God hates me.
- **F:** Anger.
- **A:** Take it out on others, rail against God.
- **R:** I hate God.

- **C:** Trial.
- **T:** Why me?
- **F:** Self-pity.
- **A:** I suffer, feel sorry for myself, compare myself to others.
- **R:** I feel picked on.

- **C:** Trial.
- **T:** This isn't fair.
- **F:** Resentment.
- **A:** I catalog past injustices, vent to others.
- **R:** I focus on the unfairness in the world.

- **C:** Trial.
- **T:** Remember me?
- **F:** Abandoned.
- **A:** I feel unworthy, stay in bed under the covers, lose trust.
- **R:** I feel forgotten. I forget my support group.

- **C:** Trial.
- **T:** What can I learn from this?
- **F:** Resilient.
- **A:** I look at the issue, seek solutions.
- **R:** I learned . . .

- **C:** Trial.
- **T:** God is helping me grow.
- **F:** Joy.
- **A:** I look for ways to help others/bless their lives.
- **R:** I become who I am capable of becoming.

Results are just another piece of information we look at to determine if we are headed in the direction we want to be going. We look at the results we are creating as a measuring stick.

The results help us answer questions like these:

- Is my life on track?
- Is this relationship healthy?
- Is the time I am spending on this worth it?
- Do I like what I am creating?
- Do I like the person I am becoming?

If we like the answers to those questions, then hallelujah!

If we *don't* like the answers to those questions, then it's back to examining what needs to be tweaked or just plain overhauled. That's not a problem. You just received some extra knowledge. Now, what are you going to do with it? Be curious. Think outside the box. Work the model backward. Start with the result you want and find out what you need to do to get it. Write down those things in the action line. How would you be feeling to inspire those actions? What is the thought that creates that emotion?

You know what you need to do.

Experiment again.

Test out your hypothesis.

Did you succeed with the result? Celebrate!

Did you fail again? Celebrate! You now have more information. You are one step closer to the result you want.

Notice that the result line should be an *I* statement. The result should not be about others. Let's go back to a previous example.

- **C:** Husband said, "You idiots! Can't you keep your Legos off the floor?"
- **T:** He shouldn't yell at the kids.
- **F:** Anger.
- **A:** I yell at my husband.
- **R:** Husband has unacceptable behavior. *(This is not an appropriate result line.)*
- **R:** I do the exact behavior I was condemning. *(This is the result line you are looking for.)*

Our models are about us. The sole purpose of the model is to help you discover more about yourself.

Consider this example. My husband came home for a dinner break one day when I was a stay-at-home mom taking care of our four children. The moment he walked in the door, I blurted out, "I am going to get a job. I cannot handle being home twenty-four-seven anymore." He responded, "Okay." Well, that was not the answer I was expecting. I wanted to blame my discontent on the children. But with my husband's response, I realized I was in control. I could get a job, or I could continue staying at home. The choice was mine.

If he had tried to extol the virtues of staying at home, I probably would have cast my blame from the children to him. My discontent could have transferred to him, and I'm sure I could have ridden that wave for years. As it was, I understood that I was in control of my experience. When I evaluated my circumstance and what I really wanted to think about it, I concluded that I wanted to be a stay-at-home mom.

I want to say it is easier to cast blame on others, but that is not a true assessment. Blame is a pattern that can repeat for years, and that road is anything but easy. A truer statement would be that it brings short-term pleasure to blame others. Blaming others means we do not need to do the changing. We do not need introspection. We just need to tell the other person what they need to do differently. Maybe it is easier. But it is not going to get you different results.

Earlier I invited you to separate your story into circumstances and thoughts. I would like to extend another invitation to separate your circumstances from your results. It is not your husband's fault you are not happy. It is not your children's fault your house is messy. It is not the Church's fault you do not have more family time. We possess so much more power than we give ourselves credit for. Too often, we hand that power over to others—our husband for our unhappiness. Our children for our messy house. The Church for inadequate family time.

Elder D. Todd Christofferson said, "The opportunity to assume personal responsibility is a God-given gift without which we cannot realize our full potential . . . personal accountability becomes both a right and a duty that we must constantly defend."[4] Taking back our power—the power to be happy, the power to have a clean home, the power to make more family time, or whatever the results we desire—may be the hard way. But most things worth doing may seem hard at the inception. Taking personal responsibility for our thoughts, feelings, actions, and results is the easier way. It is a peaceful way.

Most of us do not even take time to think about the results we want in our lives. We are on auto-pilot as the days turn into months and the months turn into years. Think about what result you want

---

4. D. Todd Christofferson, "Free Forever, to Act for Themselves," *Ensign*, November 2000.

in your life. (To get started, see Appendix: Results I Want). Make a list. Choose one. Too often we set a handful of goals in January and by the time February rolls around, we lose all our momentum. Practice constraint. Focus on one result you want. Decide what you need to do to accomplish it. Decide how you want to feel and think about it.

Is this easy-peasy? No. You can rest assured there will be obstacles along the way. That is a given. Maybe it will be your timeline. Maybe it will be your skillset. Most assuredly it will be some thoughts. But you can plan ahead by anticipating what some of those obstacles will be and creating a game plan to manage them.

Let's look at a few examples.

Result: Be on time for appointments.

OBSTACLES	GAME PLAN
Trying to fit in too much in one day.	Practice scheduling my time. Move extra things to the following day or week. Say no if my schedule is packed.
My thought: I'm always late.	Practice new thoughts that are believable and true: I get to appointments on time 75 percent of the time OR I am becoming a person who is on time.
Lose track of time.	Set an alarm for thirty minutes before I have to leave as a reminder. Get in the car within five minutes after hearing the alarm.

Result: Write a book.

OBSTACLES	GAME PLAN
My thought: I don't have anything to say.	Make a thought ladder with that thought at the bottom. Write the thought I want to believe at the top of the ladder. Fill in the other rungs and practice gradually changing my thoughts. I have a lot to say.
Feeling: Unmotivated.	Commit to sitting in front of the computer for fifteen minutes even if it is to stare at a blank screen.
Don't know where to start.	Do some research. Check out articles online. Get a writing coach.

This is your life. You are the main character. The results you create in life are dependent on *you*!

Have you read many author biographies? They are full of achievements but rarely list disappointments. We all have those results that felt like failures. We keep those swept under the rug and try to put our best face to the world.

Even the greats, the scripture heroes, faced obstacles as they tried to live up to the "holy calling . . . given . . . before the world began" (2 Timothy 1:9). Consider these examples:

- Eli restrained not his sons. Result: Eli honored his sons more than the Lord (see 1 Samuel 3–4).
- Aaron made an idol and worshipped it. Result: Aaron lost focus (see Exodus 32).
- Joseph Smith repeatedly asked the Lord's permission to allow Martin Harris to take 116 of the translated pages. Result: Joseph lost the privilege of translating for a season (see D&C 3).

Earlier I said that our results are the consequences of our actions. I know this doesn't surprise you. If you are old enough to read this book, you are old enough to know that sometimes we do not like the results of our actions. Elder Christofferson went on to say, "My plea is simply to take responsibility and go to work so that there is something for God to help us with."[5] He knows. We have our work to do, and He has His work.

The 2021 youth theme was, "Wherefore, be not weary in well-doing, for ye are laying the foundation of a great work. And out of small things proceedeth that which is great. Behold, the Lord requireth the heart and a willing mind" (D&C 64:33–34). As I put together 150 kits for the young women in our stake, I had a lot of time to think about this scripture. Cutting and packaging seemed like a small thing. Was what I was doing really going to make a difference? Was I getting weary as I measured and cut and traced and stuffed sealable bags? While what I was doing felt like the work, I realized that the compiling was not the "great work" at all. I am. I am God's "great work." The "great work" wasn't selling the farm so the Book of Mormon could be printed. The "great work" was Martin Harris.

The Lord can accomplish the organizing of His church. He can convert souls to the gospel. He can build temples. He says, "I am able to do mine own work" (2 Nephi 27:21). His great work is us. Me and you. We are the great work. It is more about who we become as we achieve our desired results. The Lord did not need the $3,000 from the sale of Martin's farm to publish the Book of Mormon. He wanted the growth, the commitment, the heart, and the willing mind. He wants us to develop characteristics so we can become the best possible version of ourselves.

I don't want to give you the impression that choosing conscious goals does not matter or that they are too much work. I do believe we are not always going to be successful. I do believe there will be obstacles along the way. I do believe some of our goals will never come to fruition. Even with all that, I LOVE goals. I love creating results in my life. I love lessons learned as I go through the pro-

---

5. Christofferson.

cess. Elder Dieter F. Uchtdorf said, "When our attention is mainly focused on our daily successes or failures, we may lose our way, wander, and fall. Keeping our sights on higher goals will help us become better."[6]

So dream big. Make big goals. And as you go through the process, watch yourself become stronger. See yourself accomplishing things you never dreamed were possible. Develop character traits that will bless you throughout eternity.

---

6. Dieter F. Uchtdorf, "You Can Do It Now!" *Ensign,* November 2013.

CONCLUSION

Before I learned this coaching model, my thoughts were the last place I went to change my experience. My thoughts felt true, so why would I try to change them? I tried all the other lines of the model first, just like you probably would:

- Maybe I need to change my circumstances.
- I hate my job. I need to get a new job.
- That friend is toxic. I am never going to speak to her again.
- This course is too hard. I should drop the class.
- I'm twenty pounds over my goal weight. I will remove all the food from the house.
- I am fifty years old. I'll lie about my age.
- The kids are driving me crazy. I'll get a job.

There is nothing wrong with getting a new job, dropping the class, or removing all the food from the house. But the truth is that new circumstances will come along. If we haven't learned how to manage our experience, then we will find ways to hate the new job, struggle with the next class, and figure out a way to make a treat from a five-year-old Jell-O packet and some hard marshmallows. We just keep running away from the hard things in life instead of learning from them and experiencing personal growth.

Consider the list above again and look at these options:

- I hate my job. I'll examine the benefits I get from it.
- That friend seems toxic; I'll get curious about her.
- This course is too hard. I'll find ways to tackle the homework.

- I'm twenty pounds over my goal weight. Confront your desire to eat by allowing the urge, but not eating.
- I am fifty years old. I will embrace the wrinkles and the achy knees.
- The kids are driving me crazy. I'll accept that some days kids make messes.

Remember that Jonah tried to run away from his circumstance. Then he found himself in another circumstance and another circumstance and another—Tarshish, the belly of a fish, Nineveh. This is the human experience. It has existed from the first human on earth and will exist to the last one.

I hope by now you believe that you have a lot more power to create your mortal experience than you give yourself credit for. The hymn "Know This, That Every Soul Is Free" comes to mind.

> Know this, that ev'ry soul is free
> To choose his life and what he'll be;
> For this eternal truth is given:
> That God will force no man to heav'n.
> He'll call, persuade, direct aright,
> And bless with wisdom, love, and light,
> In nameless ways be good and kind,
> But never force the human mind.[1]

For a while I practiced the thought, "God is in charge." It invited feelings of peace. That thought stopped serving me when I started thinking I was nothing more than a pawn in some predetermined plan. God is not in charge when I exercise my agency. I am in charge of liking or not liking another human being. I am in charge of what I choose to learn. I am in charge of the foods I eat.

Carolyn G. Depp said, "The Savior's atonement reminds us that real freedom is freedom of attitude. One may be bound in chains, whipped, enslaved, and mocked. He may lose freedom of move-

---

1. "Know This, That Every Soul is Free," *Hymns* (Salt Lake City, UT: The Church of Jesus Christ of Latter-day Saints, 1981), 240.

ment, expression, and religion. But there is one freedom that no man on earth has power to control or confiscate—each person's freedom to determine his reaction or response to a given circumstance."[2] I am in charge of that! If I can experience joy in this life, then I am probably going to be able to experience joy in the next life. That is my work.

When changing my circumstances did not work, I attempted to change my actions:

- I need more money. I'll work harder.
- I'm not feeling connected to my spouse. We'll go on more dates.
- I have wrinkles. I'll apply wrinkle cream.
- I've gained weight. I'll work out more.
- I have low self-worth. I'll try to accomplish more.
- I'm bored. I'll plan a vacation.

Again, there's nothing wrong with taking more action. Just remember that the actions are not the cure. Boredom will return after the vacation. Getting a degree and making six figures will not increase your intrinsic worth or make you happier. When I tackle my to-do list, I get a quick dopamine hit when I accomplish a lot. A quick dopamine hit is not really what I'm after in life. I am after the long-lasting joy that comes from living up to my potential.

Living up to my potential does not occur when I change my circumstance. Living up to my potential does not occur when I do more. Could living up to my potential be impacted by the way I am feeling?

Spending time examining my emotions was not the most comfortable place to spend time. I have spent a lifetime trying to live in the comfort zone of emotions. I seriously spent a big chunk of time worrying I would become a zombie if I practiced these tools, not realizing my comfort emotions were already keeping me in a robotic state. Once I realized that, what did I have to lose?

---

2. Carolyn G. Depp, "Freedom Beyond Circumstance," *Ensign*, February 1986.

Consider the following:

- It is comfortable to repeat the same argument over and over with a loved one. It is familiar. Who would have known that changing the trajectory of the interaction would not only make one less of a zombie but that the pendulum would swing to contentment and love?
- Who would have known that the fear of speaking up in a group keeps one paralyzed and zombie-like? Feeling the fear and speaking up anyway swings the pendulum to integrity and trust.
- Who would have known that suppressing grief keeps one in an unconscious, zombie-like state while allowing the heart-wrenching loss and sadness to be felt opens the door to peace and acceptance?

I turned into more of a human and less of a zombie when I opened the door to lean into all the emotions.

Proverbs 23:7 says, "As he thinketh in his heart, so is he." Does that mean that living up to my potential involves managing my thoughts?

When I learned that my thoughts were the cause of my ailments, I began to focus on them. I asked myself questions like these:

- What happened that cultivated that belief?
- Why did I interpret that experience that way?
- I cannot believe I let that thought in the driver's seat of my life.
- I just need to change my thought.

I felt a heavy weight now that I knew I was responsible for my life and how I interpreted it. Understanding that my thoughts create my experience is an empowering piece of knowledge but also a heavy burden when using it to examine the past. Then I would catch myself and remind myself that *knowledge is a heavy burden when examining the past* is just a thought. And it was a thought that was not helping me at all.

When I got better at being more deliberate about my thoughts, then I would notice when others were having thought problems.

Oh, if he would just think differently, then he would be much happier. Doesn't she know that her thoughts are causing all her problems?

Then I was back to square one, thinking thoughts I did not want to be thinking. Wasn't I better than that? Hadn't I progressed at all?

My thoughts would spiral downward again. I judged my thoughts. I questioned my ability to think differently. And I judged the rate of my perceived forward motion. Thought work is not as simple as flipping a switch. We have spent many years of our life practicing thoughts, and it is only through repetition and practice that new thoughts can emerge. And so I continued to practice.

After spending much time on each line of the model, I began to understand the power of influence for each component. Our thoughts, feelings, and actions are each important, and each of them plays an integral part in living up to our potential.

Every line of the model is important and deserves introspection and examination. I recently pondered three scriptures that seemed to relate to what I was trying to accomplish with the model.

> And I looked, and, lo, a Lamb stood on the mount Sion, and with him an hundred forty and four thousand, having his Father's name written in their **foreheads**. (Revelation 14:1; emphasis added)

> I would that ye should remember to retain the name written always in your **hearts**. (Mosiah 5:12; emphasis added)

> And he hath on his vesture and on his **thigh** a name written, KING OF KINGS, AND LORD OF LORDS. (Revelation 19:16; emphasis added)

What does it mean for me to have His name written on my forehead? My heart? My thigh? If His name is written on my forehead, does it mean I am thinking of Him constantly, trying to think as He thinks? If His name is written on my heart, am I trying to cultivate healthy emotions? Am I loving Him and loving my fellow man?

If His name is written on my thigh, am I taking action? Doing what needs to be done? Not just learning, but putting what I am learning into practice?

When we are willing to partake in some introspection, we discover new insights. New knowledge provides hope—hope that our future can be more joyful than we can imagine.

Learning about the power within has helped me understand some of those doctrines that seemed out of reach—doctrines like these:

- "Love your enemies, bless them that curse you, do good to them that hate you, and pray for them which despitefully use you, and persecute you" (Matthew 5:44).
- Forgive "seventy times seven" (Matthew 18:22).
- "Unto him that smiteth thee on the *one* cheek offer also the other; and him that taketh away thy cloak forbid not *to take thy* coat also" (Luke 6:29).
- "Be ye therefore perfect, even as your Father which is in heaven" (Matthew 5:48).

Self-coaching has helped me see the possibility of leaning into those doctrines. I understand that love is a choice. Feeling or withholding love is not a reward or a punishment we experience based on someone else's behavior. We can choose love at any time. The human experience invites mistakes, and withholding forgiveness hurts only the unforgiving.

Choosing to listen to other perspectives doesn't mean I agree with those differing perspectives. It just means I am open to other people's experiences and am willing to learn more about other beliefs and to be stronger in my convictions or open to change. This life is a journey to be enjoyed. In Paul's sermon to the Corinthians, he said, "I am exceeding joyful in all our tribulations" (2 Corinthians 7:4). This was not a thought I ever entertained. I am getting closer to believing it is possible. Realizing I am in charge of what I believe has been an empowering discovery for me. If God says it is possible to joy in our tribulations, then of course it is possible. It may take some altering of our thoughts, but I believe that with God all things are possible. I can almost wrap my brain around it when I think those trials are getting me closer and closer to being the kind of person that can be in God's presence because that does sound like a rather joyful occasion.

My parting counsel is taken from my wise friend Paul—"for I have learned, in whatsoever state I am, therewith to be content" (Philippians 4:11). You are fine just where you are. There is no hurry to be different. Embrace where you are. If you want to make changes, then lean into it and be prepared to have some growing pains and pleasures along the way.

APPENDIX

Thought Ladder

You decide you want to change your thought, but the thought you entertain the most is so believable—and the thought you want to adopt is so unbelievable. What can you do to get from one thought to the other? Create a thought ladder. Start with the thought that is believable on the bottom rung of your ladder. Then put the thought you want to believe on the top rung of the ladder. Fill the rungs in between with thoughts that take you one step closer to believing what you want to believe. Each thought, each rung, needs to be believable and needs to stretch you a little bit more.

Examples:

- I am grateful for this job.
- This job is serving a purpose.
- This job provides a way for me to pay the bills.
- I'm glad I have income.
- I hate my job.

- I am learning how to be merciful.
- I want to be merciful.
- I can be a positive part of his life.
- He is family.
- I can give him a second chance.
- I do not want to be manipulated by him.

- My timing is always perfect.
- I like the way I am balancing my life.
- I have planned for this.
- I make an effort to schedule my time.
- I did do enough.
- I did not do enough and that is okay.
- I am not doing enough.

Circumstances and Thoughts 1

Circle the circumstances and underline the thoughts in the following scripture:

> And Eliab his eldest brother heard when he spake unto the men; and Eliab's anger was kindled against David, and he said, Why camest thou down hither? and with whom hast thou left those few sheep in the wilderness? I know thy pride, and the naughtiness of thine heart; for thou art come down that thou mightest see the battle.
>
> And David said, What have I now done? *Is there* not a cause?
>
> And he turned from him toward another, and spake after the same manner: and the people answered him again after the former manner.
>
> And when the words were heard which David spake, they rehearsed *them* before Saul: and he sent for him.
>
> And David said to Saul, Let no man's heart fail because of him; thy servant will go and fight with this Philistine.
>
> And Saul said to David, Thou art not able to go against this Philistine to fight with him: for thou *art but* a youth, and he a man of war from his youth. (1 Samuel 17:28–33)

Answer Key

CIRCUMSTANCE	THOUGHT
Eliab is David's eldest brother.	Eliab's anger was kindled against David.
Eliab said, "Why camest thou down hither? With whom hast thou left those few sheep? I know thy pride, and the naughtiness of thine heart. Thou art come down that thou mightest see the battle."	
David said, "What have I now done? Is there not a cause?"	
They rehearsed them [the words] before Saul.	
Saul sent for him.	
David said, " Let no man's heart fail because of him; thy servant will go and fight with this Philistine."	
Saul said, "Thou art not able to go against this Philistine to fight with him: for thou art but a youth, and he a man of war from his youth."	

There's only one thought here because this excerpt is basically very factual. We know that anything that is said by another person can be classified as a circumstance. The thoughts occur when we *interpret* what was said. So while Saul thought that David was not a viable option to fight Goliath, he said that, so it is a circumstance.

What we are curious to know is what David's resulting thoughts were. He may have thought one or more of these:

- I will show him.
- I know God will help me.
- He can't tell me what I am capable of doing.

But since the scripture doesn't specify any of David's thoughts, we can only imagine what he thought.

I put *Eliab's anger was kindled against David* in the thought column because it is probably the author's interpretation. We're tempted to think it is factual because we would be angered if our little brother thought he was up to fighting a warrior, but it's not part of the facts in the scriptural account.

Circumstances and Thoughts 2

Write about a recent experience.

_____

_____

_____

_____

_____

_____

_____

_____

_____

_____

_____

_____

_____

_____

_____

_____

_____

Now go back and circle the circumstances and underline your thoughts.

Thought Download

There is no right or wrong way to do this. The main objective is to just get what is in your head written on paper.

Having said that, here are a few download suggestions:

- **Story download:** Write about a specific experience and what you thought about it. (Extended family dinner. Date night. The birthday gift from your husband.)
- **Stream of consciousness:** Just write down whatever comes to mind. (I wish she wouldn't have done that. I need to get some bananas from the store. I am not sure if I paid that bill yet. I don't know if I'm going to have time to call her back.)
- **List:** Create a bulleted list based on something you have been thinking about. (Family vacation ideas. How to help my son learn how to drive. Purchases I would like to make in the coming year.)
- **Topical:** Choose a specific theme and write down where your mind wanders. (Goals. Mother-in-law. Finances.)

The benefit of writing your thoughts down is that you can look at each sentence independently of the others. I have tried to do this before without paper and pen. You may not have this kind of experience, but I found that when I don't write my thoughts down, I become the judge before I act as the scribe. I justify my thoughts, defend my thoughts, or shame my thoughts before they can even get out of my head. Here's how that might play out:

- I probably shouldn't have said that to her. (It is fine. She needed to hear it.)
- My mother shouldn't have said that about me. (But maybe it is true.)
- My husband said that he was going to be home for dinner at 5:30, and it's now 6:30. (I'm probably just overreacting. I am sure he is fine and will be home soon.)

Write your thoughts down. Don't edit them. Let them flow. Then you can become the observer and think about them more objectively.

Decide which ones are recurring thoughts, thoughts that you do not enjoy, and surprising thoughts. Then you can take them through the self-coaching process.

Feelings

Accepting Affectionate Angry Anxious Authentic Awkward
Bitter Bored Brave
Carefree Combative Compassionate Controlling Cooperative
Curious
Daring Defensive Disappointed
Ecstatic Expansive
Focused Frightened
Gloomy Gracious Grouchy
Heartbroken Hotheaded Humble
Impatient Incompetent Insecure Intolerant
Jealous Joyous
Lonely Loud
Mellow Miserable
Nervous
Observant Obsessive
Paranoid Patient Phony Present
Quarrelsome Quiet
Rebellious Remorseful Responsible
Sarcastic Sensitive Sincere Spontaneous Steady Stubborn Supportive
Tactless Thankful Timid Tolerant Trusting
Uncomfortable Understanding Unsure
Victimized Vulnerable Weak Withdrawn Wonderful

Results I Want

Make a list of results you want. Include all kinds of results—serious results. Fun results. Outrageous results. Results you have not thought about for years. As you make your list, include results you have already created in your life. This will remind you about your ability to create results in your life. It will also allow you the opportunity to feel gratitude for the results you have already created.

Sample Goal Flow Chart

Goal: Write down one goal you want to accomplish.

Enter the thoughts that come up when you think about your goal.

Thought	Thought	Thought

Enter the feelings that come from the specific thought.

Feeling	Feeling	Feeling

List actions the feeling creates.

Actions	Actions	Actions

List the results from those actions.

Result	Result	Result

Goal: Write a book.

The thoughts that come up when I think about my goal:

I don't know where to start.	This will be so fun.	You don't have anything to say.

Feelings I create with those thoughts:

Confused	Excited	Doubtful

Actions the feeling creates:

• Excessive reading on other writers' processes • Procrastinate • Start . . . and then stop • Ask others their opinions	• Schedule time to write • Make it a priority • Allow myself to ponder • Think about how readers will benefit from the information • Share what I am writing with others	• Second guess myself • Confirming thoughts • Listen to my inner critic • Jump from book idea to book idea • Diminish my ideas

Results from those actions:

I never even start.	I write the book.	I never write the book.

ABOUT THE AUTHOR

Lori Holyoak and her eternal companion have four married children and seven grandchildren.

While attending her oldest daughter's college graduation, Lori felt a rekindled desire to get her own degree. At forty-four years of age, she enrolled in Brigham Young University's bachelor of general studies program and earned an English degree.

Passionate about learning and personal development, Lori seized the opportunity to receive certification at The Life Coach School. *Self-Coaching* is a culmination of her love of writing, her discipleship, and her desire to share coaching tools with those seeking to navigate life's journey.